THE PEANUTS TRIVIA
& REFERENCE BOOK

Monte Schulz and Jody Millward

An Owl Book
Henry Holt and Company | New York

For Karin and Steve, with a smile

Introduction and text copyright © 1986 by Monte Schulz and Jody Millward

Comic strips and art copyright © 1986 by United Feature Syndicate, Inc.
Based on the PEANUTS® comic strip by Charles M. Schulz

Published by Henry Holt and Company, Inc.,
521 Fifth Avenue, New York, New York 10175.

Distributed in Canada by Fitzhenry & Whiteside,
195 Allstate Parkway, Markham, Ontario L3R 4T8.

Library of Congress Catalog Card Number: 86-81208

ISBN 0-8050-0072-0 (pbk.)

First Edition

Printed in the United States of America
1 3 5 7 9 10 8 6 4 2

ISBN 0-8050-0072-0

Contents

Where Are the Answers?

Almost all the questions in this book can be answered by strips found in the following *Peanuts Parade* titles—a notation after each question indicates which book contains the answer.

1. Who's the Funny-Looking Kid with the Big Nose?
2. It's a Long Way to Tipperary
3. There's a Vulture Outside
4. What's Wrong with Being Crabby?
5. What Makes You Think You're Happy?
6. Fly, You Stupid Kite, Fly!
7. The Mad Punter Strikes Again
8. A Kiss on the Nose Turns Anger Aside
9. Thank Goodness for People
10. What Makes Musicians So Sarcastic?
11. Speak Softly, and Carry a Beagle
12. Don't Hassle Me with Your Sighs, Chuck
13. There Goes the Shutout
14. Always Stick Up for the Underbird
15. It's Hard Work Being Bitter
16. How Long, Great Pumpkin, How Long?
17. A Smile Makes a Lousy Umbrella
18. My Anxieties Have Anxieties
19. It's Great to Be a Super Star
20. Stop Snowing on My Secretary
21. Summers Fly, Winters Walk
22. The Beagle Has Landed
23. And a Woodstock in a Birch Tree
24. Here Comes the April Fool!
25. Dr. Beagle and Mr. Hyde
26. You're Weird, Sir!
27. Kiss Her, You Blockhead!
28. I'm Not Your Sweet Babboo!
29. The Way of the Fussbudget Is Not Easy

Other *Peanuts* books available from Henry Holt and Company:

You Don't Look 35, Charlie Brown!
Big League *Peanuts*
And the Beagles and the Bunnies Shall Lie Down Together:
    The Theology in *Peanuts*
Classroom *Peanuts*
Things I Learned After It Was Too Late (And Other Minor Truths)
Things I've Had to Learn Over and Over and Over
    (Plus a Few Minor Discoveries)
Snoopy's Tennis Book
The Snoopy Festival
Snoopy and the Twelve Days of Christmas

Introduction

The cartoonist, the experienced and successful one, is just another long-distance runner whose achievements are measured only in the distance where both stamina and talent come together to create a special kind of genius. In the case of *Peanuts*, the achievement is seen easily in thirty-five years of daily and full-page Sunday strips and the dozens of characters and hundreds of situations brought to life within them. We know because, in putting this book together, we read almost every strip published in those thirty-five years, and if there was any one thing that caught our attention, it was this variety found in an otherwise seemingly small and circumscribed comic-strip world.

From the beginning, we wanted this book to serve as something more than another entry in the current trivia sweepstakes. We think of it not only as a good game book—something fun to play around with—but also as a reference work on thirty-five years of *Peanuts*. In keeping with that idea, we tried to come up with a variety of questions covering everything from classrooms and sandlots to summer camp, Linus's pumpkin patch, Lucy's psychiatric booth, and Snoopy's eccentric imagination. Most of the *Peanuts* characters' major activities and obsessions over the past thirty-five years are covered by the questions we ask.

We had a great time doing this book. Reading through thousands of strips, searching for the ones that would make good trivia questions, was every bit as much fun as it sounds. But more than just providing us a good time, reading the old strips again gave us something else as well: memories of moments and events in our own lives that were marked by or mirrored in the strip. We were not surprised. *Peanuts*, after all, has always served as a unique and acute reflection of our culture and the changing times. Looking back at the strips gave us a chance to reflect on who we were and what we were about when Sally was born, when the Great Pumpkin first appeared, and when Snoopy took to the skies in search of the Red Baron. For us, and perhaps for you, this trivia book also serves as a scrapbook of sorts: a collection of particularly poignant memorabilia for those sympathetic to the problems of that little roundheaded kid.

One last note for the truly avid fan of the strip: Don't feel bad if you can't answer every question in this book. We stumped the Cartoonist himself five times!

Monte Schulz
Jody Millward
Santa Barbara, 1986

Special acknowledgment: Tagging each one of the almost three hundred strips that we eventually chose, and having to photocopy and collate them all, would have been considerably less enjoyable without the help of our tireless assistant, Carol A. Shelley. We would not have wanted to do this without her. Thanks, Carol!

Dreams and Schemes

1. Which pumpkin patch does the Great Pumpkin visit on Halloween night?

(Dr. Beagle and Mr. Hyde)

1.

LINUS, YOU REMEMBER EUDORA, DON'T YOU?

SURE... HOW ARE YOU?

HALLOWEEN IS COMING!

ON HALLOWEEN NIGHT THE GREAT PUMPKIN RISES OUT OF THE PUMPKIN PATCH AND BRINGS TOYS TO ALL THE CHILDREN IN THE WORLD

BUT FIRST HE LOOKS OVER ALL THE PUMPKIN PATCHES TO SEE WHICH ONE IS THE MOST SINCERE..IF HE CHOOSES THIS PUMPKIN PATCH, I'LL GET TO MEET HIM!

THIS YEAR I JUST KNOW HE'S GOING TO CHOOSE THIS PUMPKIN PATCH!! I JUST KNOW IT!

OH, WHAT A GLORIOUS MOMENT THAT WILL BE!!!

SEE?

HOW SHARPER THAN A SERPENT'S TOOTH IS A SISTER'S "SEE?"

2. What kind of plane does Snoopy fly?

(It's a Long Way to Tipperary)

_____

3. Where is the World's Wrist Wrestling Championship held?

(My Anxieties Have Anxieties)

_____

4. Why was Snoopy disqualified from the World's Wrist Wrestling Championship?

(My Anxieties Have Anxieties)

_____

5. Who is usually Snoopy's mixed doubles partner?

(Kiss Her, You Blockhead!)

2.
HERE'S THE WORLD WAR I FLYING ACE ZOOMING THROUGH THE AIR IN HIS SOPWITH CAMEL!
DOWN BELOW I CAN SEE THE INFANTRYMEN HUDDLED IN THEIR MUDDY TRENCHES...
POOR BLIGHTERS!
WE FLYING ACES ALWAYS CALL THEM "POOR BLIGHTERS"
SCHULZ

3.
" SEVENTH ANNUAL WORLD'S WRIST WRESTLING CHAMPIONSHIP"
YOU SHOULD ENTER, SNOOPY... IT'S GOING TO BE HELD ON MAY 3rd IN PETALUMA..
"PETALUMA"?
SCHULZ
THE DEFENDING CHAMPION STANDS SIX FOOT THREE AND WEIGHS 333 POUNDS..
"PETALUMA"?!

4.
WHAT ARE YOU DOING HOME? WHAT HAPPENED IN PETALUMA?
?
"OFFICIAL RULES AND REGULATIONS OF WRIST WRESTLING... THE CONTESTANTS FACE EACH OTHER GRASPING THE BASE OF EACH OTHER'S THUMB AND...
I WAS DISQUALIFIED... I DON'T HAVE A THUMB!
SCHULZ

5.
HEY, PARTNER, IT'S ME, MOLLY VOLLEY!
?
THERE'S A MIXED DOUBLES TENNIS TOURNAMENT THIS WEEK...I HOPE YOU'RE IN GOOD SHAPE...
I KNOW I'VE GAINED WEIGHT, BUT IF YOU SAY ANYTHING, I'LL HIT YOU OVER THE HEAD WITH MY RACKET!
WHEN I KNOW I COULD GET HIT OVER THE HEAD WITH A RACKET, I CAN BE THE SOUL OF DISCRETION!
SCHULZ

_____

6. What does Snoopy do every year on Veterans Day?

(Here Comes the April Fool!)

_____

6.

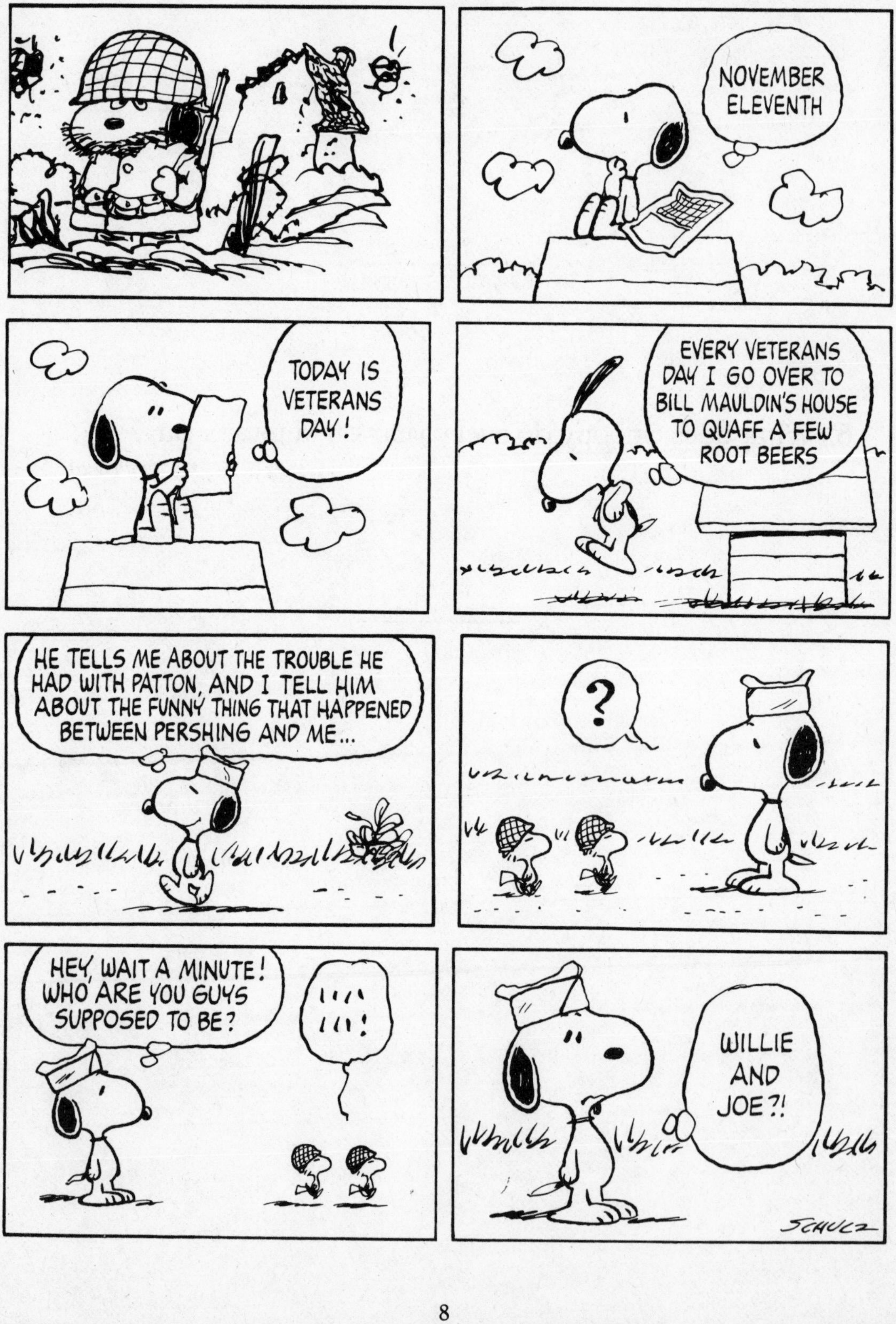
NOVEMBER ELEVENTH
TODAY IS VETERANS DAY!
EVERY VETERANS DAY I GO OVER TO BILL MAULDIN'S HOUSE TO QUAFF A FEW ROOT BEERS
HE TELLS ME ABOUT THE TROUBLE HE HAD WITH PATTON, AND I TELL HIM ABOUT THE FUNNY THING THAT HAPPENED BETWEEN PERSHING AND ME...
?
HEY, WAIT A MINUTE! WHO ARE YOU GUYS SUPPOSED TO BE?
WILLIE AND JOE?!
SCHULZ

7. What did Woodstock discover at the bottom of Snoopy's water dish?

   (I'm Not Your Sweet Babboo!)

   _____

8. How did Charlie Brown save Snoopy from the icicle that had him trapped in his doghouse?

   (Thank Goodness for People)

   _____

9. What is the name of the country club where Marcie and Peppermint Patty caddy?

   (The Beagle Has Landed)

   _____

10. Who was the "Mad Punter"?

   (What Makes Musicians So Sarcastic?)

7.

YOUR RESEARCH HAS TOLD YOU WHAT ?
THERE'S A VESSEL FROM THE WAR OF 1812 LYING AT THE BOTTOM OF MY WATER DISH ?
I HATE MYSELF FOR DOUBTING HIS RESEARCH
SCHULZ

8.

I'M DOING JUST WHAT THE MAN FROM THE HUMANE SOCIETY SAID TO DO...
SNIF? SNIF? SNIF?
?
SNOOPY
ZOOM
WHAM!
SAVED BY A PIZZA!
GOOD GRIEF!
SCHULZ

9.

THIS MUST BE THE COUNTRY CLUB, SIR
I THINK YOU'RE RIGHT, MARCIE
PRETTY FANCY ENTRANCE! REAL STONE PILLARS AND A GENUINE BRASS NAME PLATE...
ACE COUNTRY CLUB
SCHULZ

10.

I DIDN'T TAKE YOUR STUPID OL' FOOTBALL!
WELL, SOMEBODY DID!
SOMEBODY'S BEEN KICKING IT ALL OVER THE NEIGHBORHOOD, AND I'D LIKE TO KNOW...
WUMP
THE "MAD PUNTER" HAS STRUCK AGAIN!
SCHULZ

---

11. What is the name of the fort guarded by the world-famous sergeant-major and his legionnaires?

(Kiss Her, You Blockhead!)

11.

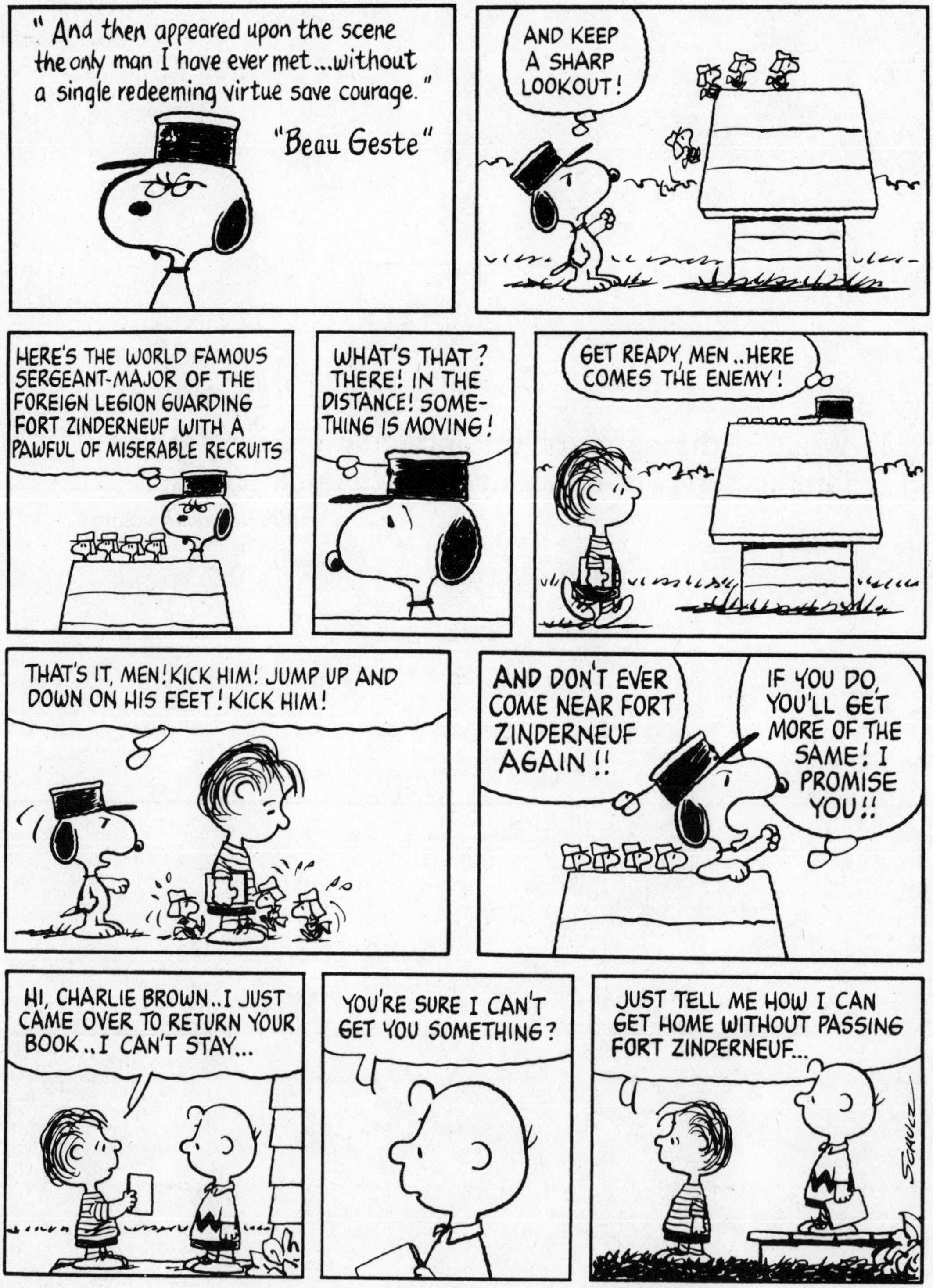

" And then appeared upon the scene the only man I have ever met...without a single redeeming virtue save courage."
"Beau Geste"
AND KEEP A SHARP LOOKOUT!
HERE'S THE WORLD FAMOUS SERGEANT-MAJOR OF THE FOREIGN LEGION GUARDING FORT ZINDERNEUF WITH A PAWFUL OF MISERABLE RECRUITS
WHAT'S THAT? THERE! IN THE DISTANCE! SOMETHING IS MOVING!
GET READY, MEN..HERE COMES THE ENEMY!
THAT'S IT, MEN! KICK HIM! JUMP UP AND DOWN ON HIS FEET! KICK HIM!
AND DON'T EVER COME NEAR FORT ZINDERNEUF AGAIN!!
IF YOU DO, YOU'LL GET MORE OF THE SAME! I PROMISE YOU!!
HI, CHARLIE BROWN..I JUST CAME OVER TO RETURN YOUR BOOK..I CAN'T STAY...
YOU'RE SURE I CAN'T GET YOU SOMETHING?
JUST TELL ME HOW I CAN GET HOME WITHOUT PASSING FORT ZINDERNEUF...
SCHULZ

12. Who reported Snoopy to the Head Beagle, and on what charge?

(It's Great to Be a Super Star)

_____

13. Who did Linus manage to convince that the Great Pumpkin exists?

(It's a Long Way to Tipperary)

_____

14. What is the name of Snoopy's airline?

(Dr. Beagle and Mr. Hyde)

_____

15. What is the opening line of Snoopy's gothic novel?

(Summers Fly, Winters Walk)

12.

YOU DID IT!! YOU REPORTED SNOOPY TO THE HEAD BEAGLE!
IT WAS HIS OWN FAULT! HE NEVER WANTED TO GO RABBIT CHASING WITH ME!
SHE REPORTED ME, AND NOW I HAVE TO APPEAR BEFORE THE HEAD BEAGLE..THIS WILL BRING DISGRACE UPON THE DAISY HILL PUPPY FARM...
IN ALL THE HISTORY OF THE DAISY HILL PUPPY FARM, NO ONE HAS EVER BEEN ORDERED TO APPEAR BEFORE THE HEAD BEAGLE!!
SCHULZ

13.

OKAY, LINUS, TELL ME ALL ABOUT THE "GREAT PUMPKIN"
WELL, IT'S LIKE THIS...
ON HALLOWEEN NIGHT, THE "GREAT PUMPKIN" CHOOSES THE PUMPKIN PATCH THAT HE THINKS IS THE MOST SINCERE... THEN HE RISES OUT OF THE PUMPKIN PATCH, AND FLIES THROUGH THE AIR BRINGING PRESENTS TO CHILDREN EVERYWHERE
I BELIEVE YOU!
YOU DO?!
FANTASTIC!
SCHULZ

14.

LADIES AND GENTLEMEN, WE WILL BE LANDING SHORTLY..THE CAPTAIN HAS TURNED ON THE "NO SMOKING" SIGN...
I HAVE?
PLEASE BE SURE YOUR SEAT IS IN AN UPRIGHT POSITION AND ALL HAND-LUGGAGE IS STORED UNDER THE SEAT IN FRONT OF YOU
IT HAS BEEN A PLEASURE SERVING YOU..THANK YOU FOR FLYING "ACE AIRLINES"... HAVE A NICE DAY!
WHERE ARE WE?
SCHULZ

15.

SNOOPY, I HAVE TO READ A BOOK THIS WEEK..
DO YOU HAVE SOMETHING GOOD?
"IT WAS A DARK AND STORMY NIGHT... SUDDENLY, A SHOT RANG OUT!"
I REALLY DON'T CARE MUCH FOR MYSTERIES...
IT'S NOT A MYSTERY, IT'S A GOTHIC!
SCHULZ

16. What strange creature was found in Woodstock's nest?

(It's Hard Work Being Bitter)

_____

17. What squadron does Snoopy fly with?

(My Anxieties Have Anxieties)

_____

18. What did Belle do while serving in France during WWI?

(You're Weird, Sir!)

_____

19. What miracle did Peppermint Patty believe she had witnessed?

(You're Weird, Sir!)

16.

I FOUND IT!
I FOUND THE STRANGE CREATURE WHO WAS IN WOODSTOCK'S NEST
THERE! WHAT DO YOU THINK OF THAT?
AN EGG?!

17.

HERE'S THE WORLD WAR I FLYING ACE OVER PONT-A-MOUSSON WITH THE EIGHTH U.S. AERO SQUADRON...
THE TIME IS 5:00 P.M. ON NOVEMBER 3, 1918... WE ARE TAKING PHOTOGRAPHS AT AN ALTITUDE OF 2200 METERS...
DOWN BELOW I CAN SEE THE POSITIONS OCCUPIED BY THE NINETY-SECOND U.S. ARMY DIVISION, AND TWO THOUSAND YARDS TO THE NORTH I CAN SEE THE GERMAN POSITIONS...
HAVE YOU EVER IN ALL YOUR LIFE SEEN SUCH GOOD RESEARCH?

18.

HEY, SPIKE! WHERE HAVE YOU BEEN? LOOK WHO'S HERE..OUR SISTER BELLE... SHE'S IN THE RED CROSS!
WE'RE ALL TOGETHER! I CAN'T BELIEVE IT!
THIS CALLS FOR A CELEBRATION...
ROOT BEER ALL AROUND!

19.

IT WAS A MIRACLE, SNOOPY
THIS BUTTERFLY LANDED ON MY NOSE, SEE, AND THEN IT TURNED INTO AN ANGEL...
I THOUGHT YOU'D BE INTERESTED BECAUSE YOU HAVE SUCH A BIG NOSE
UP UNTIL THEN I WAS INTERESTED

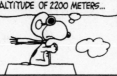

20. Which of Snoopy's novels features Joe Eskimo and his polar cow?

(It's Hard Work Being Bitter)

20.

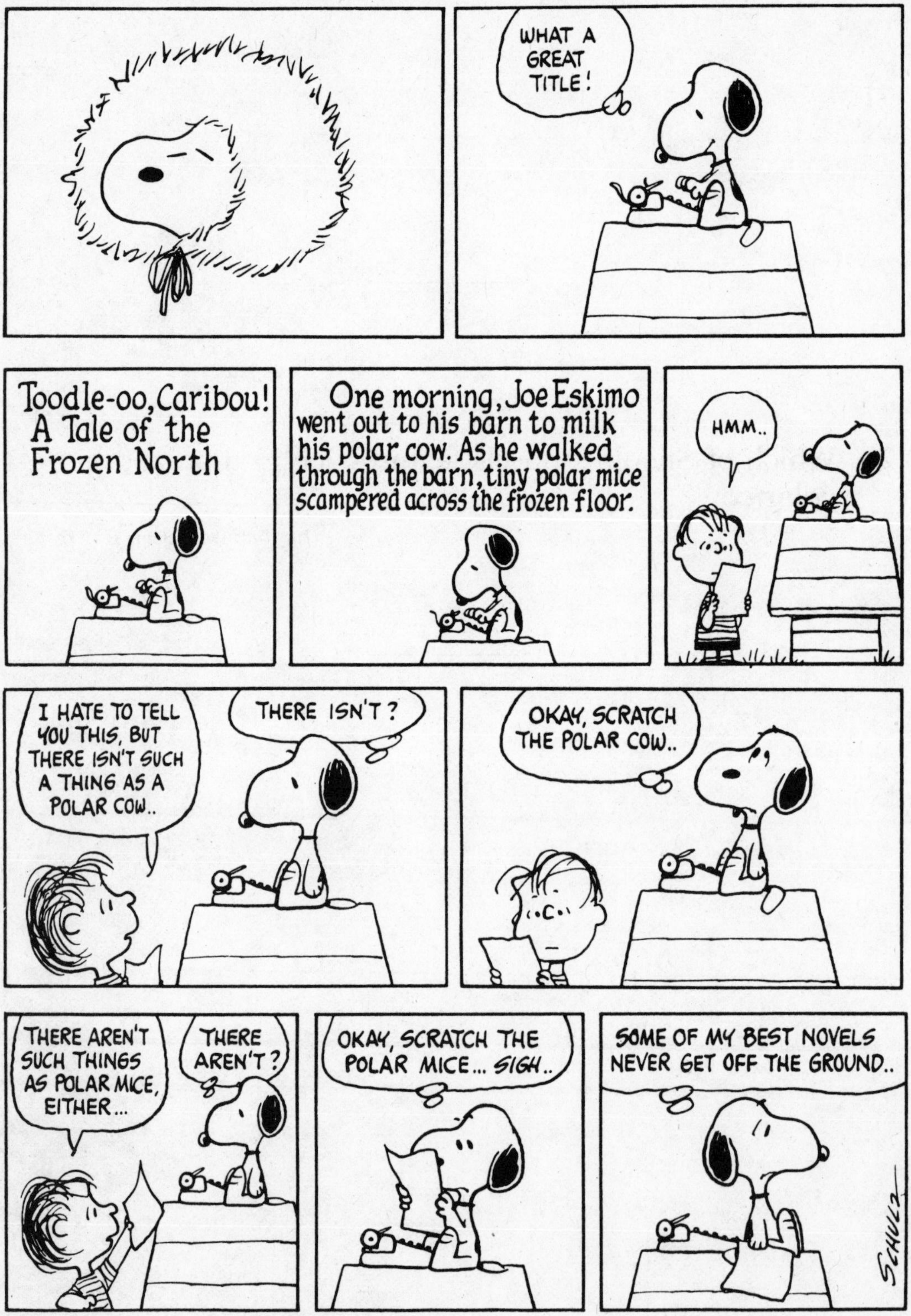
WHAT A GREAT TITLE!
Toodle-oo, Caribou! A Tale of the Frozen North
One morning, Joe Eskimo went out to his barn to milk his polar cow. As he walked through the barn, tiny polar mice scampered across the frozen floor.
HMM..
I HATE TO TELL YOU THIS, BUT THERE ISN'T SUCH A THING AS A POLAR COW..
THERE ISN'T?
OKAY, SCRATCH THE POLAR COW..
THERE AREN'T SUCH THINGS AS POLAR MICE, EITHER...
THERE AREN'T?
OKAY, SCRATCH THE POLAR MICE... SIGH..
SOME OF MY BEST NOVELS NEVER GET OFF THE GROUND..
SCHULZ

21. What are Lucy's credentials as a psychiatrist?

(A Smile Makes a Lousy Umbrella)

_____

22. What coded message did Snoopy receive from the Head Beagle?

(It's Hard Work Being Bitter)

_____

23. What magazine bought all of Snoopy's Kitten Kaboodle stories?

(Speak Softly and Carry a Beagle)

_____

24. Whose parents took her from Linus's pumpkin patch to have her deprogrammed?

(The Beagle Has Landed)

21.

PSYCHIATRIC HELP 5¢
BEFORE WE BEGIN, I'D LIKE TO ASK YOU SOMETHING...
THE DOCTOR IS IN
WHAT ARE YOUR CREDENTIALS?
I KNOW EVERYTHING!
THE DOCTOR IS IN
THOSE ARE GOOD CREDENTIALS!
THE DOCTOR IS IN

22.

YOU GOT A CODED MESSAGE FROM THE HEAD BEAGLE?
CAN YOU READ IT? HAVE YOU FIGURED IT OUT? WHAT DOES IT SAY?
I CAN'T BELIEVE IT...
"THOMPSON IS IN TROUBLE!"
THAT STUPID THOMPSON! HE'S DONE IT AGAIN!!
THOMPSON?! WHO IS THOMPSON?

23.

And so, once again, Kitten Kaboodle had to admit she had been outsmarted by a dog.
An ordinary dog at that.
DO YOU THINK THERE'S A MARKET FOR ANTI-CAT STORIES?
"PLAYBEAGLE" HAS BOUGHT THE WHOLE SERIES!

24.

HAVE YOU EVER BEEN "DEPROGRAMMED," SIR?
IT'S TERRIBLE! MY FAMILY HAS BEEN YELLING AT ME ALL NIGHT...
APPARENTLY IT'S ALL RIGHT TO BELIEVE IN SANTA CLAUS, BUT IT'S WRONG TO BELIEVE IN THE "GREAT GRAPE"
I THINK THAT'S "PUMPKIN," MARCIE...
I'M STILL FEELING A LITTLE DIZZY....

Friends and Lovers

1. Who first called Charlie Brown "wishy-washy"?

   (There Goes the Shutout)

   ———————

2. Who is madly in love with Linus?

   (What Makes Musicians So Sarcastic?)

   ———————

3. Who was Peppermint Patty's date for the Valentine's Day dance?

   (Dr. Beagle and Mr. Hyde)

   ———————

4. Who rescued Charlie Brown and Snoopy when they got lost in a blizzard?

   (Dr. Beagle and Mr. Hyde)

1.
?
CHARLIE BROWN IS AN EASY GOING SORT OF FELLOW, ISN'T HE ?
I'LL SAY HE IS... GOOD OL' CHARLIE BROWN...
HE SEEMS TO GET ALONG WITH EVERYBODY
NOBODY HATES HIM...
EVERYBODY LIKES HIM...
WHAT A WISHY-WASHY CHARACTER!
SCHULZ

(Patty)

2.
LUCY'S LOOKING FOR ME, SALLY..
BUT DON'T TELL HER WHICH WAY I WENT, OKAY?
THANK YOU!
SIGH I'D DO ANYTHING FOR THAT MAN!
SCHULZ

3.
THAT WAS THE BEST VALENTINE'S DAY EVER, PIG-PEN!
I HAVEN'T HAD SO MUCH FUN AT A DANCE IN ALL MY LIFE!
SMAK!
WOW!
SCHULZ

4.
MARCIE, I CAN'T WALK THIS WAY..THE COMIC BOOKS ARE COMING APART AGAIN
LOOK, SIR! I THINK I SEE SOMEBODY!
CHUCK! HOW'D YOU FIND US? WE'VE BEEN LOOKING ALL OVER FOR YOU!
WE JUST FOLLOWED THE PAGES FROM SOME COMIC BOOKS...

5. When Charlie Brown was in the hospital, what two friends held a vigil on the park bench outside his window?

(Here Comes the April Fool!)

5.

IF YOU SIT ON A PARK BENCH ACROSS FROM THE HOSPITAL AND STARE UP AT HIS WINDOW, THE PATIENT GETS BETTER...

POOR CHUCK..I HATE TO THINK OF HIM LYING UP THERE IN THAT HOSPITAL ROOM

YOU KIND OF LIKE CHUCK, DON'T YOU, SIR?

WELL, I..YOU KNOW... I FEEL SORT OF..YOU KNOW...HE..I...HE..

I LOVE CHUCK! I THINK HE'S REAL NEAT!

REAL NEAT? YOU THINK HE'S REAL NEAT?

I SURE DO! SOMEDAY I HOPE HE'LL ASK ME TO THE SENIOR PROM!

IN FACT, IF HE ASKED ME, I'D EVEN MARRY CHUCK!

COME WITH ME, MARCIE

IS THIS THE EMERGENCY ENTRANCE, MA'AM? WE'RE FRIENDS OF CHARLES BROWN

I HAVE ANOTHER PATIENT FOR YOU.. I THINK SHE'S SICKER THAN HE IS!

6. To whom did Linus give his security blanket?

(And a Woodstock in a Birch Tree)

_____

7. When Charlie Brown went on vacation, who took care of Snoopy?

(It's Great to Be a Super Star)

_____

8. What mistake did Charlie Brown's father make when he cut Peppermint Patty's hair?

(Speak Softly and Carry a Beagle)

_____

9. Who told Charlie Brown, "You're the nicest person I've ever known"?

(Kiss Her, You Blockhead!)

6.
YOU DID WHAT?
I GAVE MY BLANKET TO EUDORA!
WHAT COULD I DO? SHE SMILED AT ME!
I'M SURPRISED AT YOU! YOU USUALLY DON'T DO DUMB THINGS LIKE THAT..
IT WAS A CUTE SMILE
SCHULZ

7.
YOU'RE SURE IT'S NOT GOING TO BE ANY TROUBLE?
OF COURSE NOT! YOU GO ON YOUR VACATION, AND SNOOPY CAN STAY WITH US...
I'LL WHIP HIM INTO SHAPE! I MEAN, I'LL TAKE GOOD CARE OF HIM...
WHAT DO YOU USUALLY FEED HIM.. A FEW CRUSTS OF STALE BREAD AND SOME WATER?
AAUGH!
SCHULZ

8.
CHUCK! LOOK AT MY HAIR!
YOU DIDN'T TELL YOUR DAD I'M A GIRL! LOOK! HE GAVE ME A BOY'S HAIRCUT!!
I CAN'T GO TO A SKATING COMPETITION LOOKING LIKE THIS!!
WAAH!!!
EASY WITH THE TEARS, PLEASE... YOU'RE MELTING MY SNOWMAN!
SCHULZ

9.
I'VE ALWAYS BEEN FOND OF YOU, CHARLES... I THINK YOU'RE THE NICEST PERSON I'VE EVER KNOWN..
I HATE TO SEE YOU SUFFER ALL THE TIME
I KNOW YOU COULD NEVER LOVE SOMEONE LIKE ME WHO WEARS GLASSES SO I'LL JUST LEAVE YOU ALONE
HOW DOES HE DO THAT?
SCHULZ

10. According to Charlie Brown, who was the first person to call him "Charlie Brown"?

(It's Hard Work Being Bitter)

10.

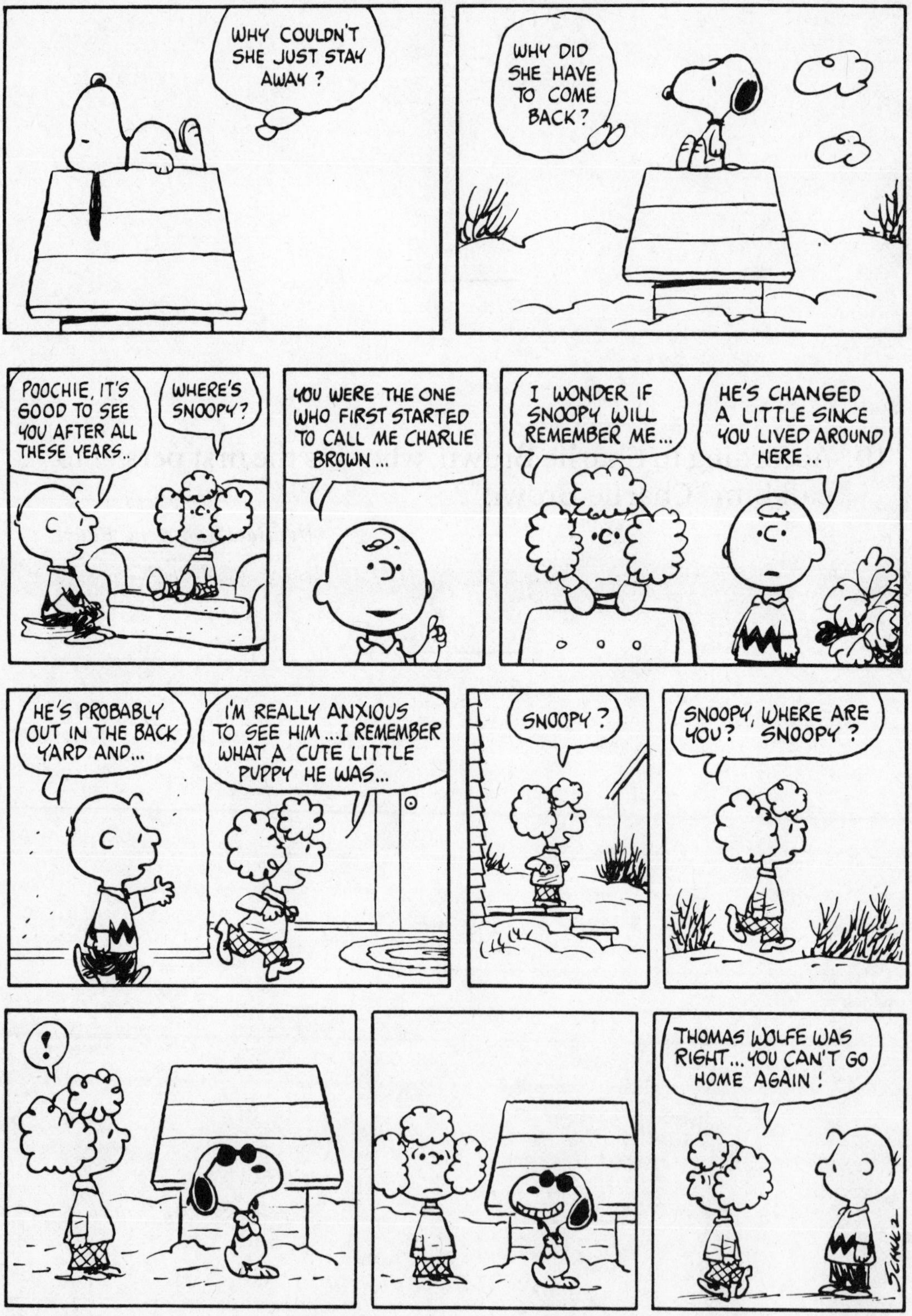

WHY COULDN'T SHE JUST STAY AWAY?
WHY DID SHE HAVE TO COME BACK?
POOCHIE, IT'S GOOD TO SEE YOU AFTER ALL THESE YEARS..
WHERE'S SNOOPY?
YOU WERE THE ONE WHO FIRST STARTED TO CALL ME CHARLIE BROWN...
I WONDER IF SNOOPY WILL REMEMBER ME...
HE'S CHANGED A LITTLE SINCE YOU LIVED AROUND HERE...
HE'S PROBABLY OUT IN THE BACK YARD AND...
I'M REALLY ANXIOUS TO SEE HIM...I REMEMBER WHAT A CUTE LITTLE PUPPY HE WAS...
SNOOPY?
SNOOPY, WHERE ARE YOU? SNOOPY?
!
THOMAS WOLFE WAS RIGHT...YOU CAN'T GO HOME AGAIN!
SCHULZ

11. When Peppermint Patty stays at Chuck's house, where does she sleep?

(How Long, Great Pumpkin, How Long?)

_____

12. Who has a pencil-pal?

(Fly, You Stupid Kite, Fly!)

_____

13. Who decided to write a book about Beethoven?

(And a Woodstock in a Birch Tree)

_____

14. What is the little red-haired girl's name?

11.

HI, CHUCK! I'M HERE! WHERE'S THE GUEST ROOM?
WELL, I THOUGHT I'D LET YOU STAY IN MY ROOM, AND I'D JUST MOVE INTO THE...
NONSENSE! I HEARD YOU HAD A LITTLE GUEST COTTAGE OR SOMETHING OUT IN BACK... C'MON, LEAD ME TO IT!
YOU SHOULD HAVE HAD THEM MAKE IT A LITTLE BIGGER, CHUCK...
SCHULZ

12.

DEAR PEN-PAL
RATS!
DEAR PEN
RATS!
DE
RATS!
DEAR PENCIL-PAL,
SCHULZ

13.

IN MY BOOK ABOUT BEETHOVEN, I'VE MADE A FEW IMPROVEMENTS
FOR INSTANCE, INSTEAD OF PLAYING THE PIANO, I HAVE HIM PLAYING AN ELECTRIC GUITAR...
ALSO, IN MY BOOK HE DOESN'T HAVE STOMACH PAINS..
I'VE UPDATED IT TO TENNIS ELBOW!
SCHULZ

14. ?!!

15. Woodstock charged Snoopy six dollars for breaking something at a party. What was it?

(It's Hard Work Being Bitter)

_____

16. What is Sally's pet name for Linus?

(You're Weird, Sir!)

_____

17. Who made Peppermint Patty's dress for the skating competition?

(Speak Softly and Carry a Beagle)

_____

18. Who tried to sell Girl Scout cookies to Snoopy?

(Speak Softly and Carry a Beagle)

15.

I SPOILED WOODSTOCK'S PARTY!

HE HAD INVITED THIS CUTE LITTLE BIRD THAT HE'S IN LOVE WITH, BUT HE NEVER GOT TO TALK WITH HER BECAUSE I TALKED WITH HER THE WHOLE EVENING!

SO HE SENT ME A BILL FOR SIX DOLLARS FOR A BROKEN HEART! OH, WOODSTOCK, MY LITTLE FRIEND OF FRIENDS...

DON'T YOU REALIZE THAT YOUR HEART IS WORTH MUCH MUCH MORE THAN SIX DOLLARS?!!

SIGH

16.

SEE THE VALENTINE I MADE FOR LINUS?

ON THE INSIDE I WROTE, "TO MY SWEET BABBOO"

HE SAYS HE'S NOT YOUR "SWEET BABBOO"

WHAT DOES HE KNOW?

17.

MARCIE! WHAT DO YOU WANT?!

I'VE BROUGHT YOU SOMETHING, SIR...

MY MOM MADE YOU A SKATING DRESS BECAUSE SHE KNEW I WASN'T REALLY GOING TO BE ABLE TO DO IT RIGHT...

SHE SAID SHE ALSO KNOWS YOU DON'T HAVE A SKATING MOTHER TO SEW OUTFITS FOR YOU, AND SHE WANTS YOU TO LOOK GOOD IN THE COMPETITION..

OH, MARCIE! MARCIE! MARCIE! MARCIE! MARCIE! MARCIE! MARCIE! MARCIE!

THAT'S MY NAME, SIR!

18.

I SEE SOMEONE!

IS IT A RESCUER? MAYBE IT'S SOMEONE COMING TO MUG ME! IT'S BAD ENOUGH BEING LOST WITHOUT GETTING MUGGED, TOO!

HE'S GETTING CLOSER! I'M TRAPPED! I'M DOOMED!!

HELLO! MY NAME IS LORETTA, AND I'M SELLING GIRL SCOUT COOKIES!

19. Who vies with Lucy for Schroeder's affection?

(There's a Vulture Outside)

19.

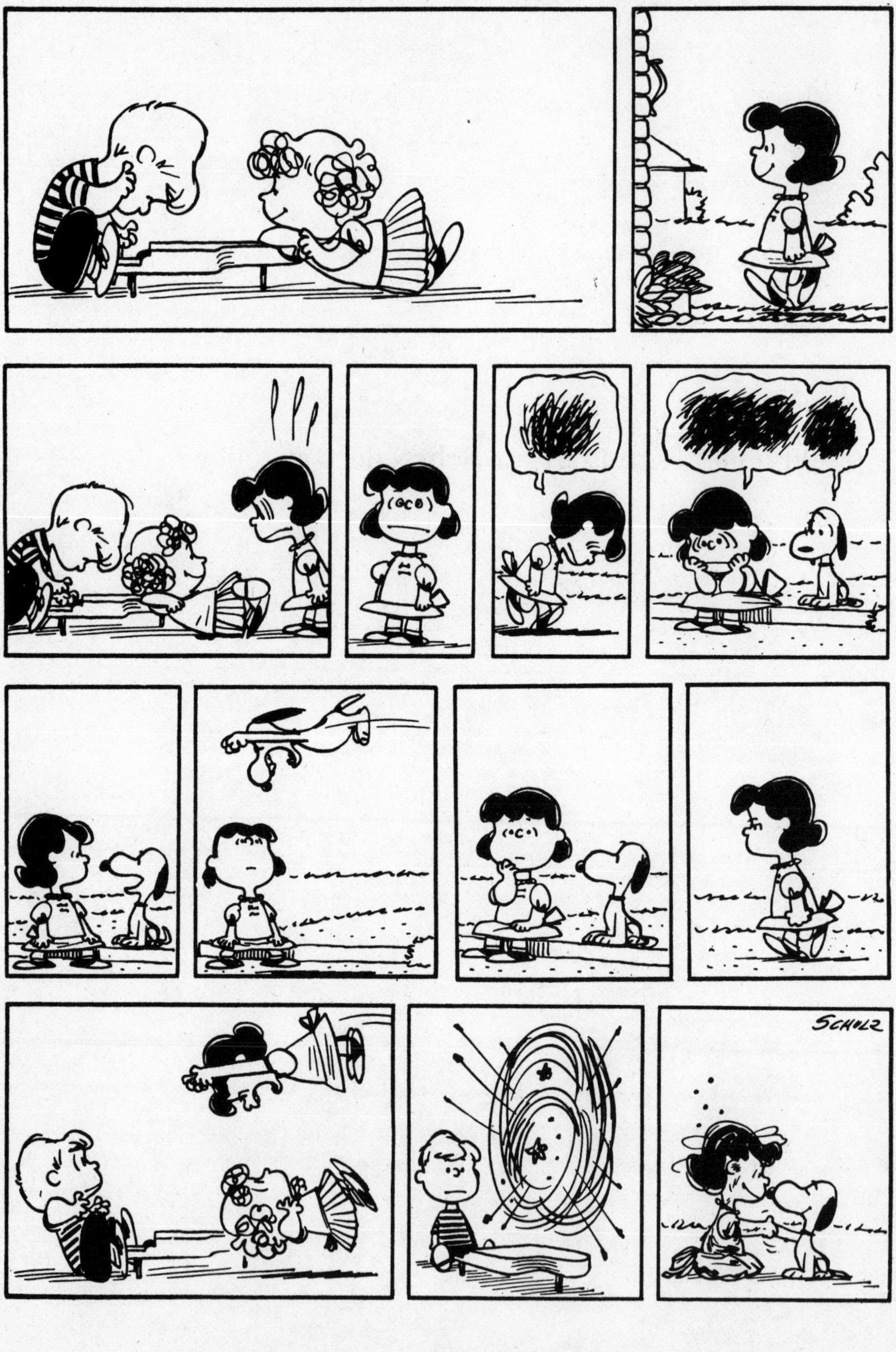
SCHULZ

20. How did Marcie and Peppermint Patty meet?

(It's Hard Work Being Bitter)

_____

21. Why did Snoopy fail to catch the burglar at Peppermint Patty's house?

(Speak Softly and Carry a Beagle)

_____

22. What instrument does Lucy insist that the man she marries must play?

(Always Stick Up for the Underbird)

_____

23. According to Charlie Brown, why can't you sleep if you have a broken heart?

(Stop Snowing on My Secretary)

20.
GOLLY, SIR, IT'S GREAT TO SEE YOU AT CAMP AGAIN THIS YEAR
STOP CALLING ME "SIR"!
DO YOU REMEMBER ME? MY NAME IS MARCIE.. WE WERE IN THE SAME TENT LAST YEAR
OF COURSE, I REMEMBER YOU...
AS SOON AS I SAW YOU GET OFF THE BUS, I SAID, "WELL, IF IT ISN'T WHAT'S-HER-FACE!"
I APPRECIATE YOUR REMEMBERING ME, SIR...
STOP CALLING ME "SIR"!

21.
WHAT KIND OF A WATCHDOG ARE YOU?!
I'M A SEASICK WATCHDOG!
GET OFF THAT WATERBED, AND CATCH THAT BURGLAR!
AUGH!
THAT STUPID CHUCK! HE CAN'T EVEN OWN A GOOD WATCHDOG!
THERE'S OUR EXCUSE... WE'LL BLAME EVERYTHING ON THE ROUND-HEADED KID!

22.
THE MAN I MARRY MUST BE TALL AND HANDSOME..
THE MAN I MARRY MUST BE STRONG AND BRAVE AND TRUE..
THE MAN I MARRY MUST KNOW HOW TO PLAY THE ACCORDION..
GOOD!

23.
HOW CAN YOU TELL IF YOU HAVE A BROKEN HEART?
WELL, FOR ONE THING, IF YOU HAVE A BROKEN HEART, YOU CAN'T SLEEP AT NIGHT..
WHEN YOU ROLL OVER IN BED, THE JAGGED EDGES POKE YOU IN THE SIDE
I'M GLAD I TALKED TO AN EXPERT

Habits and Hobbies

———

1. What is Linus's security blanket made of?

(There Goes the Shutout)

———

1.

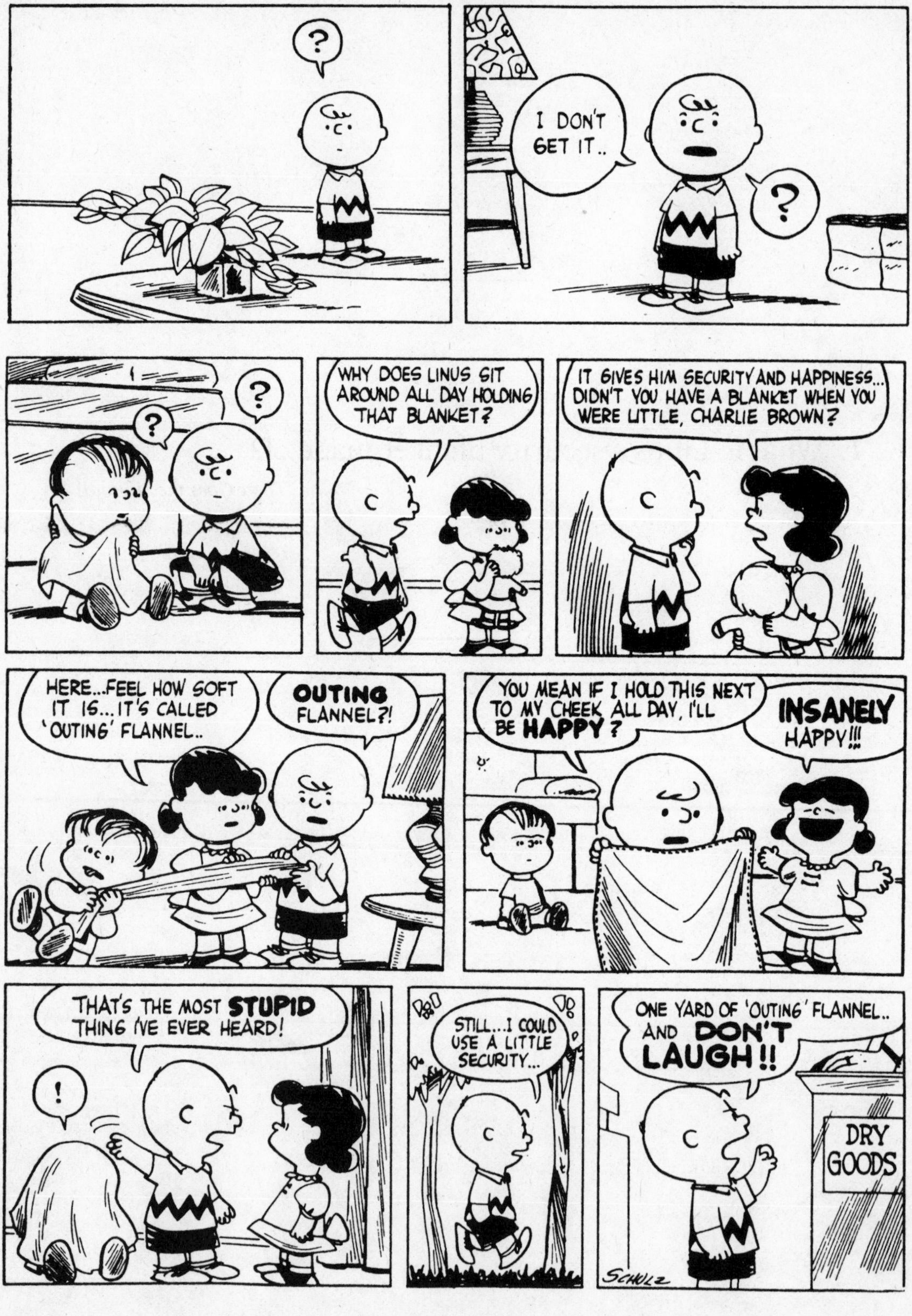
?
I DON'T GET IT..
?
?
?
WHY DOES LINUS SIT AROUND ALL DAY HOLDING THAT BLANKET?
IT GIVES HIM SECURITY AND HAPPINESS... DIDN'T YOU HAVE A BLANKET WHEN YOU WERE LITTLE, CHARLIE BROWN?
HERE...FEEL HOW SOFT IT IS...IT'S CALLED 'OUTING' FLANNEL..
OUTING FLANNEL?!
YOU MEAN IF I HOLD THIS NEXT TO MY CHEEK ALL DAY, I'LL BE HAPPY?
INSANELY HAPPY!!!
THAT'S THE MOST STUPID THING I'VE EVER HEARD!
!
STILL...I COULD USE A LITTLE SECURITY...
ONE YARD OF 'OUTING' FLANNEL.. AND DON'T LAUGH!!
DRY GOODS
SCHULZ

2. What instrument does Charlie Brown play?

(Peanuts)

_____

3. What instrument, and type of music, does Snoopy play?

(What Makes You Think You're Happy?)

_____

4. Who introduced Schroeder to the piano?

(Peanuts)

_____

5. What company makes Schroeder's pianos?

(Speak Softly and Carry a Beagle)

2.

HOW WOULD YOU LIKE TO HAVE ME ACCOMPANY YOU ON MY CIGAR-BOX BANJO, SCHROEDER?
PLINK PLANK PLINK PLANK PLINK
PLINK PLANK PLINK PLANK PLINK PLINK
?
SCHULZ

3.

YOU WANT TO HEAR SOME **REAL** MUSIC? LISTEN TO THIS!
POLKAS, SCHOTTISHES AND WALTZES
POLKAS, SCHOTTISHES AND WALTZES
SEE? THAT'S REAL MUSIC! THAT'S THE SORT OF MUSIC THAT PEOPLE LIKE! NOT THAT OL' BEETHOVEN STUFF!
I CAN'T STAND IT! I JUST CAN'T STAND IT!
POLKAS, SCHOTTISHES AND WALTZES POLKAS, SCHOTTISHES AND WALTZES
SCHULZ

4.

SEE HOW EASY IT IS, SCHROEDER?
PLINK PLINK PLINK
THE PIANO IS A BEAUTIFUL INSTRUMENT IF PLAYED PROPERLY
PLINK PLINK PLINK
NOW LET'S HEAR YOU PLAY, HUH, SCHROEDER?
SCHULZ

5.

HELLO... "ACE" PIANO COMPANY?
I WANT TO ORDER ANOTHER PIANO... MY FIRST ONE WAS CHEWED UP BY A KITE-EATING TREE ... THIS LAST ONE WAS THROWN DOWN A SEWER...
YES, I WANT THE SAME KIND AS BEFORE...
TAKE YOUR TIME ON DELIVERY!!
SCHULZ

6. According to Snoopy, why do dogs chase cars?

(The Mad Punter Strikes Again)

———————

7. Who first caused Charlie Brown to miss the football?

(Peanuts)

———————

8. Who made two sport coats out of Linus's blanket?

(Stop Snowing on My Secretary)

———————

9. What great Impressionist's work does Snoopy own?

(What's Wrong with Being Crabby?)

6.

ARF ARF ARF
WHY DO DOGS CHASE CARS?
IT'S QUITE OBVIOUS...
TO TRY TO READ THE LETTERING ON THE HUB CAPS!
SCHULZ

7.

HE'LL KICK MY HAND! I JUST KNOW HE WILL!
I CAN'T GO THROUGH WITH IT!
?
YOU DIDN'T KICK THE BALL, CHARLIE BROWN... WHY DIDN'T YOU KICK IT?
SCHULZ

8.

HE HAD MY BLANKET MADE INTO A SPORT COAT! I'M GOING CRAZY!
I GAVE YOU THAT BLANKET TO KEEP FOR ME ONLY TO SEE IF I COULD GIVE IT UP, AND YOU HAD IT MADE INTO A SPORT COAT!
NOT A SPORT COAT...
TWO SPORT COATS!
SCHULZ

9.

I'LL CHECK TO SEE IF THE WATER HURT ANY OF YOUR THINGS, SNOOPY..
I DON'T THINK THERE WAS TOO MUCH DAMAGE..THE TV STILL WORKS..EVERYTHING SEEMS OKAY
OH, AND HERE'S GOOD NEWS FOR YOU...
YOUR VAN GOGH WASN'T HARMED A BIT!
WHAT A RELIEF!
SCHULZ

10. In what sport did Charlie Brown win a trophy?

(There's a Vulture Outside)

10.

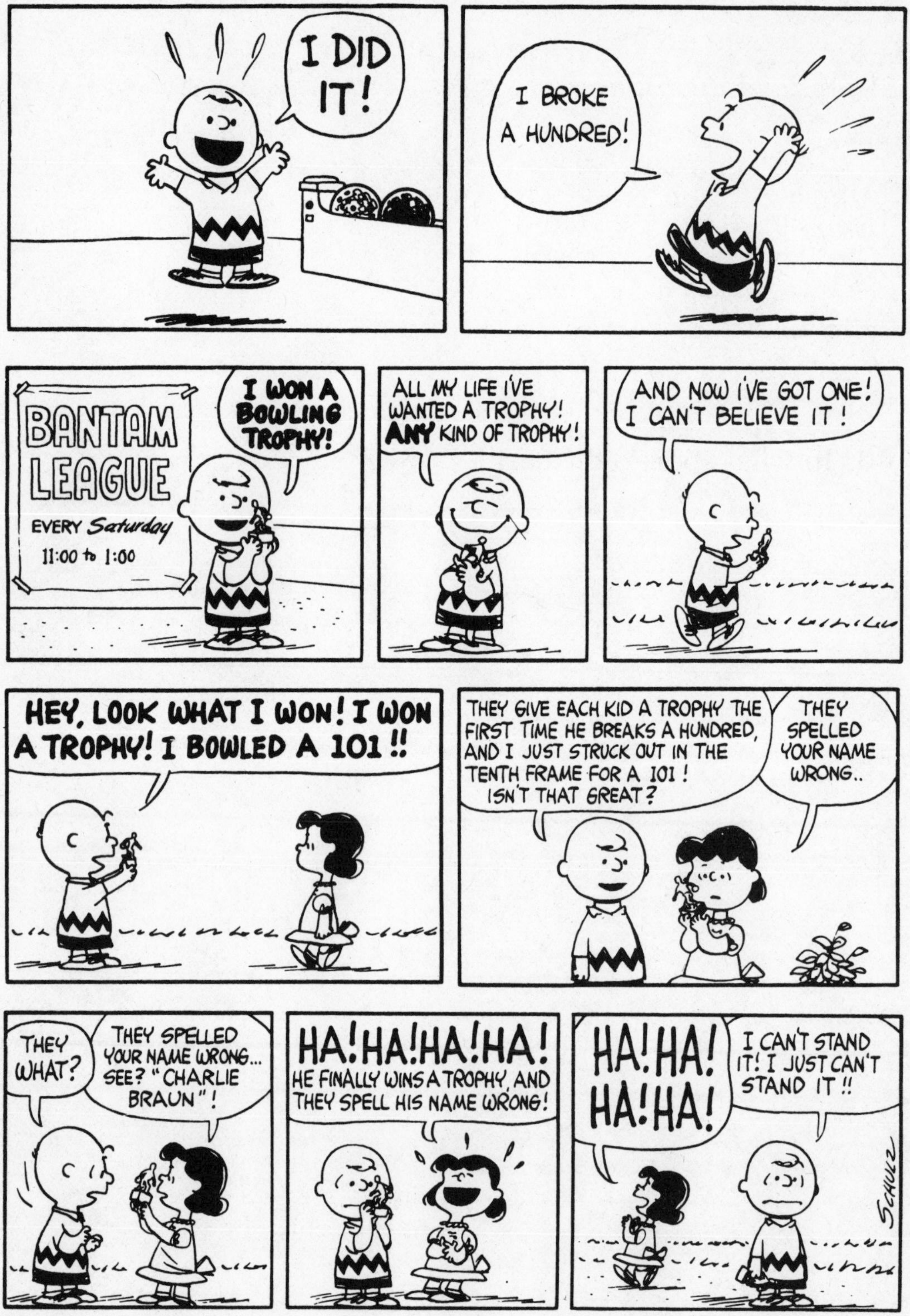
I DID IT!
I BROKE A HUNDRED!
BANTAM LEAGUE
EVERY Saturday
11:00 to 1:00
I WON A BOWLING TROPHY!
ALL MY LIFE I'VE WANTED A TROPHY! ANY KIND OF TROPHY!
AND NOW I'VE GOT ONE! I CAN'T BELIEVE IT!
HEY, LOOK WHAT I WON! I WON A TROPHY! I BOWLED A 101!!
THEY GIVE EACH KID A TROPHY THE FIRST TIME HE BREAKS A HUNDRED, AND I JUST STRUCK OUT IN THE TENTH FRAME FOR A 101! ISN'T THAT GREAT?
THEY SPELLED YOUR NAME WRONG..
THEY WHAT?
THEY SPELLED YOUR NAME WRONG... SEE? "CHARLIE BRAUN"!
HA! HA! HA! HA! HE FINALLY WINS A TROPHY, AND THEY SPELL HIS NAME WRONG!
HA! HA! HA! HA!
I CAN'T STAND IT! I JUST CAN'T STAND IT!!
SCHULZ

11. Who rescued Linus's blanket from the cat next door?

(And a Woodstock in a Birch Tree)

_____

12. Who took up jogging?

(Summers Fly, Winters Walk)

_____

13. Who likes to pat birds on the head?

(There's a Vulture Outside)

_____

14. If the black keys are just painted on Schroeder's toy piano, how does he manage to play difficult pieces?

(There Goes the Shutout)

11.

I CAN'T BELIEVE YOU SURVIVED A FIGHT WITH THE CAT NEXT DOOR
YOU NOT ONLY WON THE FIGHT, BUT YOU RESCUED THAT KID'S STUPID BLANKET
I'D LOVE TO HEAR HOW YOU DID IT...
BUT NOT IN DETAIL
SCHULZ

12.

I HAVE A SURPRISE FOR YOU..
AS LONG AS YOU'RE INTO JOGGING, I THOUGHT YOU MIGHT LIKE TO HAVE A REAL JOGGING SUIT
HERE... SEE HOW IT FITS...
IT MAY BE A LITTLE BIG...
SCHULZ

13.

PAT PAT PAT PAT
SIGH!
WHAT IN THE WORLD DO YOU THINK YOU'RE DOING?!
DO YOU REALIZE THAT PEOPLE ARE COMING UP TO ME, AND SAYING, "YOUR BROTHER PATS BIRDS ON THE HEAD"? WELL, I WANT YOU TO STOP IT! DO YOU HEAR ME?! STOP IT!!!
TRIP!
SCHULZ

14.

I WAS JUST NOTICING SOMETHING, SCHROEDER...AREN'T THE BLACK KEYS ON YOUR PIANO JUST PAINTED ON?
YES,.. I GUESS SO...
WELL, MAYBE THIS IS A FOOLISH QUESTION, BUT IF THOSE KEYS ARE JUST PAINTED ON, HOW DO YOU PLAY ALL THOSE DIFFICULT PIECES?
I PRACTICE A LOT!
SCHULZ

15. Who were Peppermint Patty's opponents in the golf-tournament?

(You're Weird, Sir!)

_____

16. Who refused to join the Snow League?

(How Long, Great Pumpkin, How Long?)

_____

17. What title did Lucy first compete for in 1952?

(There Goes the Shutout)

_____

18. Why did Peppermint Patty lose the skating competition?

(Stop Snowing on My Secretary)

15.

SORRY, JOE RICHKID... YOUR DRIVE JUST WENT OUT OF BOUNDS...

SORRY, MASKED MARVEL... YOUR DRIVE JUST WENT OUT OF BOUNDS...

SORRY, PATRICIA... YOUR DRIVE JUST WENT OUT OF BOUNDS...

THIS IS THE SORRIEST GROUP I'VE EVER SEEN!

16.

HA! I GUESS I SHOWED YOU GUYS!

I BUILT MY OWN SNOWMAN IN MY OWN BACKYARD, AND I DID IT WITHOUT BELONGING TO A TEAM OR A LEAGUE OR ANYTHING!

WHO CARES? WE'RE INTO BOWLING NOW! WE HAVE SPONSORS AND TROPHIES AND DINNERS AND EVERYTHING!

I HOPE YOU MISS THE FIVE PIN!!

AND MAY ALL YOUR SPLITS BE SEVEN-TEN!

17.

MY MOTHER THINKS I'M WONDERFUL!

I IMAGINE SHE DOES, LUCY...

SHE THINKS I'LL BE A CINCH TO WIN THE TITLE...

WHAT TITLE?

"MISS FUSS-BUDGET OF 1952"

YOUR MOTHER IS A SHREWD JUDGE OF CHARACTER, LUCY

SHE THINKS I'M WONDERFUL

18.

YES, MA'AM... I'M HERE FOR THE SKATING COMPETITION...

SKATERS *Register* HERE!

HOW ABOUT PRACTICE TIME, MA'AM? NOW? GOOD! I'LL PUT MY SKATES ON...

WHAT ARE YOU LOOKING AT, KID?!

YOUR SKATES... I THINK YOU'VE MADE A LITTLE MISTAKE

THIS IS A ROLLER SKATING COMPETITION!

52

19. Who lost eight thousand checkers games in a row, and to whom?

(There Goes the Shutout)

19.

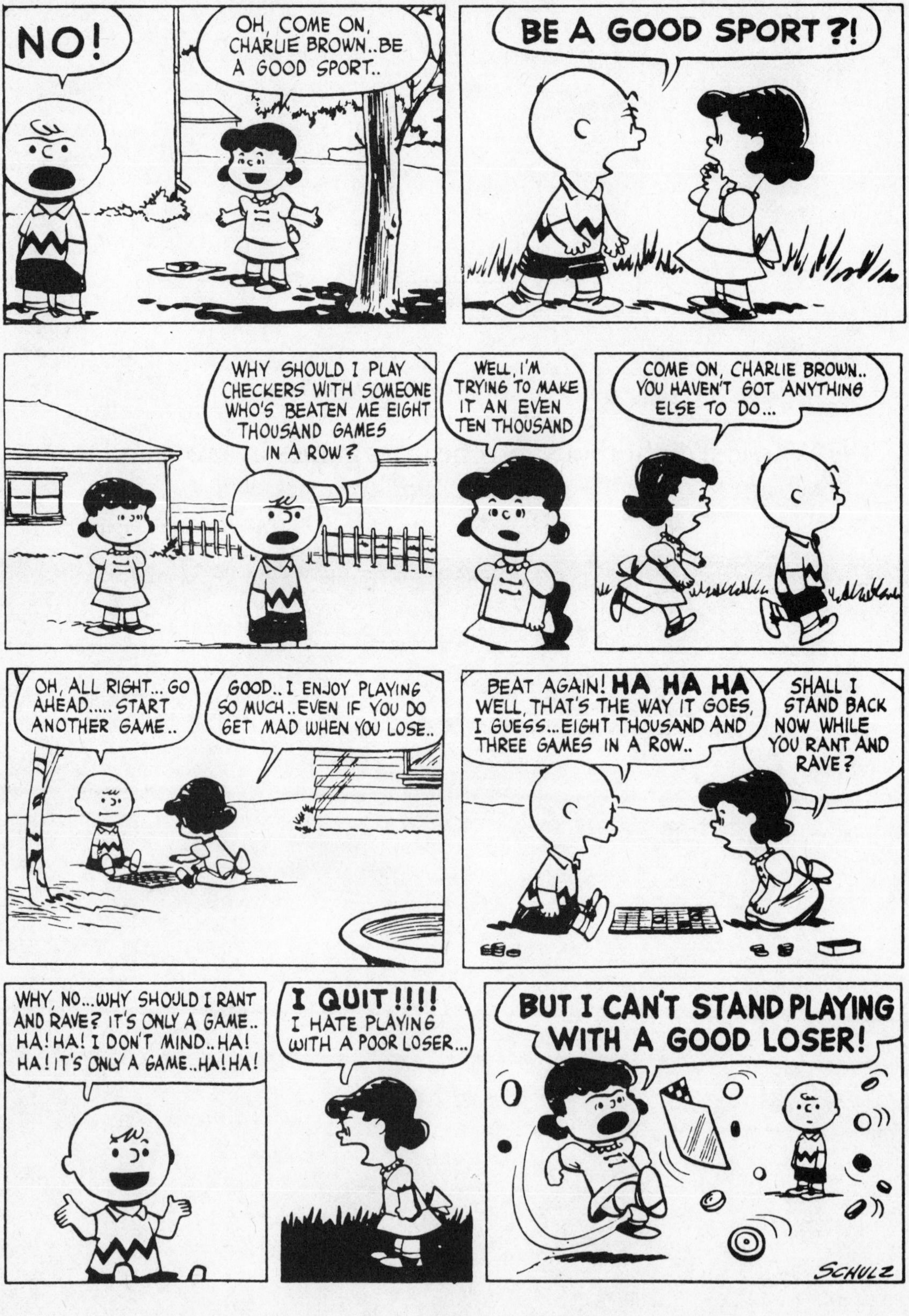
NO!
OH, COME ON, CHARLIE BROWN..BE A GOOD SPORT..
BE A GOOD SPORT?!
WHY SHOULD I PLAY CHECKERS WITH SOMEONE WHO'S BEATEN ME EIGHT THOUSAND GAMES IN A ROW?
WELL, I'M TRYING TO MAKE IT AN EVEN TEN THOUSAND
COME ON, CHARLIE BROWN.. YOU HAVEN'T GOT ANYTHING ELSE TO DO...
OH, ALL RIGHT... GO AHEAD..... START ANOTHER GAME..
GOOD.. I ENJOY PLAYING SO MUCH..EVEN IF YOU DO GET MAD WHEN YOU LOSE..
BEAT AGAIN! HA HA HA WELL, THAT'S THE WAY IT GOES, I GUESS...EIGHT THOUSAND AND THREE GAMES IN A ROW..
SHALL I STAND BACK NOW WHILE YOU RANT AND RAVE?
WHY, NO...WHY SHOULD I RANT AND RAVE? IT'S ONLY A GAME.. HA! HA! I DON'T MIND..HA! HA! IT'S ONLY A GAME..HA! HA!
I QUIT!!!!! I HATE PLAYING WITH A POOR LOSER...
BUT I CAN'T STAND PLAYING WITH A GOOD LOSER!
SCHULZ

Summer Camp

1. What summer camp does Woodstock go to?

(Stop Snowing on My Secretary)

———————

2. One year Charlie Brown's tentmate had an answer for everything. What was that answer?

(Stop Snowing on My Secretary)

———————

3. What camper calls Peppermint Patty "Sir"?

(How Long, Great Pumpkin, How Long?)

———————

4. Who attended beanbag camp one summer?

(Kiss Her, You Blockhead!)

1.

AH, ANOTHER LETTER FROM WOODSTOCK WHO'S AT EAGLE CAMP

"DEAR FRIEND OF FRIENDS... TODAY WE HEARD A SPECIAL LECTURE BY A CATERPILLAR WHO HAD CRAWLED ALL THE WAY ACROSS A FREEWAY WITHOUT GETTING RUN OVER.."

2.

THERE'S THE CALL FOR DINNER..

I WONDER IF MY 'TENTMATE HEARD IT...I'D BETTER SEE...

HEY, PAL...IT'S DINNERTIME!

SHUT UP AND LEAVE ME ALONE!

3.

ARE YOU SURE THIS IS ALL RIGHT, SIR?

STOP CALLING ME "SIR"! OF COURSE, IT'S ALL RIGHT!

I CHECKED US OUT WITH OUR COUNSELOR, AND SHE SAID JUST TO MAKE SURE WE'RE BACK BY NINE

WHO ARE WE GOING TO SEE?

WELL, ONE OF THE BOYS IS NAMED CHUCK AND THE OTHER ONE IS KIND OF A FUNNY LOOKING KID WITH A BIG NOSE, BUT HE'S REAL NEAT

I APPRECIATE YOUR TAKING ME WITH YOU, SIR...

STOP CALLING ME "SIR"!

4.

I GOT A LETTER FROM MY SISTER SALLY... SHE'S AT "BEANBAG" CAMP

"BEANBAG" CAMP?

ALL THEY DO IS LIE IN THEIR BEANBAGS, AND WATCH TV AND EAT JUNK FOOD

MORE POTATO CHIPS, PLEASE!

5. Who wrote to Charlie Brown from summer camp?

(I'm Not Your Sweet Babboo!)

_____

6. What is Floyd's affectionate nickname for Marcie?

(Summers Fly, Winters Walk)

_____

7. Where did Snoopy take his troop for a photo hike?

(I'm Not Your Sweet Babboo!)

_____

8. The summer Charlie Brown was elected camp president, what nickname did they give him, and why?

(How Long, Great Pumpkin, How Long?)

5.

Dear Charles, Only one more day of camp. Then we can be together again.
Hi, Chuck! Tomorrow we go home. How about me coming over to see you?
Dear Marcie and Patty, I won't be here when you get home.
I have enlisted in the Navy for two hundred years.
SCHULZ

6.

GOOD MORNING, LAMBCAKE
ALL RIGHT, FLOYD, CUT IT OUT!
CAN'T YOU GET IT THROUGH YOUR HEAD THAT MARCIE DOESN'T WANT ANYTHING TO DO WITH YOU?
BUT I LIKE HER! I THINK SHE'S BEAUTIFUL!
WELL, MARCIE?
WHAP HIM WITH A WAFFLE, SIR...HE'S BEING SARCASTIC AGAIN!
SCHULZ

7.

I JUST SAW YOUR STUPID DOG GO BY... WHERE'S HE GOING?
HE'S TAKING HIS FRIENDS TO "POINT LOBOS" ON A PHOTO HIKE...
"POINT LOBOS"?! DOESN'T HE KNOW HOW FAR THAT IS? HOW'S HE EVER GOING TO FIND IT?
IF IT'S THERE WHEN WE GET THERE, WE'LL KNOW WE'RE THERE
SCHULZ

8.

CONGRATULATIONS, KID!
?
YEAH, GOOD GOING, SACK! YOU'VE JUST BEEN ELECTED CAMP PRESIDENT!
CONGRATULATIONS, SACK!!!
"SACK"?!
SCHULZ

9. Which Beagle Scouts got married at Point Lobos?

(I'm Not Your Sweet Babboo!)

_____

10. What does Harriet always bring along on the Beagle Scout hikes?

(Dr. Beagle and Mr. Hyde)

_____

11. Who got thrown in jail when the Beagle Scouts went out for a night on the town?

(Dr. Beagle and Mr. Hyde)

_____

12. What new friend did Sally initiate into the pleasures of camp life?

(And a Woodstock in a Birch Tree)

9.

OKAY, GANG, IT'S TIME TO HEAD BACK HOME
WHO'S NOT GOING?
BILL AND HARRIET? WHY AREN'T THEY GOING? THEY'RE GETTING WHAT?
MARRIED?!!!...
SCHULZ

10.

WHEN WE GET TO THE TOP OF THE HILL, WE'LL ALL EAT THE ANGEL FOOD CAKE THAT HARRIET BROUGHT
WHAT?
WHY CAN'T WE EAT THE CAKE AT THE TOP OF THE HILL?
"BECAUSE HARRIET ATE IT AT THE BOTTOM OF THE HILL!"
SCHULZ

11.

SO YOU GUYS ALL WENT INTO TOWN, AND GOT IN A BRAWL...WHAT ABOUT HARRIET? WHERE'S HARRIET?
IN JAIL?!
WOW! I GUESS I HEARD YOU WRONG..I THOUGHT YOU SAID "IN JAIL," AND SO MY EARS WENT UP AND MY HAT FLEW OFF...
IN JAIL?!
SCHULZ

12.

WELL, I SUPPOSE YOU HAD YOUR USUAL MISERABLE TIME AT CAMP...DID YOU HATE IT?
UNFORTUNATELY, NO! I MET A NEW GIRL THERE NAMED EUDORA
I HAD TO KEEP CONVINCING HER THAT CAMP WAS FUN...
MY MISERABLE TIME WAS RUINED!!
SCHULZ

13. Where did Charlie Brown hide to avoid going to summer camp?

(Speak Softly and Carry a Beagle)

---

14. Why was Charlie Brown sent home early from camp?

(It's Hard Work Being Bitter)

---

15. What happened when Peppermint Patty met the little red-haired girl at camp?

(It's Hard Work Being Bitter)

---

16. Why was Woodstock kicked out of Eagle Camp?

(Stop Snowing on My Secretary)

13.

I SORT OF FIGURED THAT YOU'D BE HERE, CHARLIE BROWN...

I TRIED TO GO TO CAMP... I REALLY DID... I WENT DOWN TO THE BUS STATION, BUT I JUST COULDN'T GET ON THE BUS...

THAT'S WHEN I CAME BACK HERE TO THE PITCHER'S MOUND... I'VE BEEN SITTING HERE FOR TWO DAYS... MAYBE I'LL SIT HERE FOR THE REST OF MY LIFE...

EVEN JOB GOT UP FROM AMONG THE ASHES EVENTUALLY...

JOB NEVER HAD TO WORRY ABOUT GOING TO SUMMER CAMP

14.

WHAT DID THE COUNSELOR SAY, CHARLIE BROWN?

I'M BEING SENT HOME.. THEY SAY THAT I'M A TROUBLEMAKER!

YOU? A TROUBLEMAKER? THAT'S RIDICULOUS !!!

THEY SAID THAT SOMETHING HAPPENED OVER AT THE GIRLS' CAMP, AND MY NAME WAS MENTIONED AND THAT OBVIOUSLY I WAS A TROUBLEMAKER SO THEY'RE SENDING ME HOME...

WE'LL SUE THEM, CHARLIE BROWN! WE'LL TAKE IT TO THE SUPREME COURT!

MY NAME WAS MENTIONED AT THE GIRLS' CAMP! WOW!!

15.

I STOOD IN FRONT OF THAT LITTLE RED-HAIRED GIRL AND I SAW HOW PRETTY SHE WAS...

SUDDENLY, I REALIZED WHY CHUCK HAS ALWAYS LOVED HER, AND I REALIZED THAT NO ONE WOULD EVER LOVE ME THAT WAY..

I STARTED TO CRY, AND I COULDN'T STOP... I MADE A FOOL OUT OF MYSELF, BUT I DIDN'T CARE! I JUST LOOKED AT HER AND I CRIED AND CRIED AND CRIED...

I HAVE A BIG NOSE AND MY SPLIT-ENDS HAVE SPLIT-ENDS, AND I'LL ALWAYS BE FUNNY-LOOKING, AND I THINK I'M GOING TO CRY AGAIN..........

16.

AH, ANOTHER LETTER FROM WOODSTOCK!

"DEAR FRIEND OF FRIENDS... I AM A FAILURE... I HAVE JUST WASHED OUT OF EAGLE CAMP... I FEEL TERRIBLE..."

"I HAD ALWAYS DREAMED OF SOMEDAY BEING AN EAGLE AND SOARING HIGH ABOVE THE CLOUDS, BUT NOW MY DREAMS ARE OVER... I WAS WASHED OUT FOR GETTING TOO MANY BEAK-BLEEDS.."

POOR WOODSTOCK!

Personals

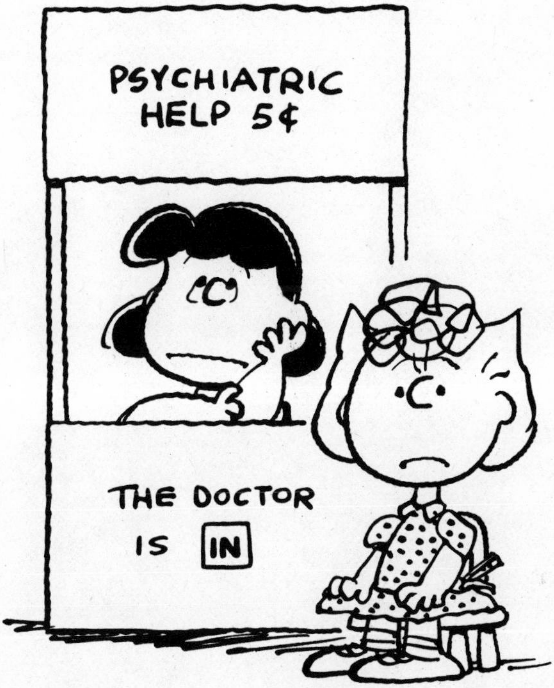
PSYCHIATRIC HELP 5¢
THE DOCTOR IS IN

1. Who were the original four characters in the strip?

(Peanuts)

_____

2. Who was the fifth character introduced in the strip?

(Peanuts)

_____

3. Who was the sixth character?

(Peanuts)

_____

1.

(*Charlie Brown, Patty, Shermy . . .*)

(*. . . and Snoopy.*)

———————

2.

———————

3.

4. What was Randolph's problem?

(I'm Not Your Sweet Babboo!)

_____

5. Who is the "human soil-bank"?

(Always Stick Up for the Underbird)

_____

6. What was the great "Snicker-Snack" slip-up?

(Always Stick Up for the Underbird)

_____

7. What is Peppermint Patty's full name?

(Stop Snowing on My Secretary)

4.

YOU SAY YOUR NAME IS RANDOLPH? OKAY, RANDOLPH, LET'S GET TO WORK...

I'M GOING TO HELP YOU TO GIVE UP YOUR BLANKET... FIRST, HOWEVER, I HAVE TO ASK YOU A FEW PERSONAL QUESTIONS..

MAY I ASK WHY YOU WEAR YOUR BLANKET OVER YOUR HEAD?

SO YOU WON'T SEE THE THREE TEDDY BEARS I'M HOLDING!

5.

ISN'T THAT 'PIG-PEN' A MESS?

LOOK AT HIS CLOTHES.. AND HIS HAIR... AND THAT DIRTY FACE..

YOU KNOW WHAT HE LOOKS LIKE? WHAT?

A HUMAN SOIL-BANK!

6.

SOMEBODY AT THE "SNICKER-SNACK" FACTORY SLIPPED UP..

THERE WAS SUPPOSED TO BE A MARBLE IN THIS BOX OF "SNICKER-SNACKS"...

LOOK WHAT HAPPENED..

FOUR HUNDRED MARBLES AND ONE 'SNICKER-SNACK'!

7.

MY NAME IS PATRICIA REICHARDT, AND I AM REPORTING TO THE STUDENT COUNCIL AS REQUESTED

I HAVE ALSO BROUGHT MY ATTORNEY WHO WILL BE ADVISING ME..

WHERE'S JOHN DOE AND RICHARD ROE? I THOUGHT THEY WERE GOING TO BE HERE..

YES, I'M PREPARED TO ANSWER ALL QUESTIONS

I THINK I SHOULD OPEN WITH AN IMPASSIONED PLEA AGAINST THE STAMP ACT

MY ATTORNEY WILL ADVISE ME OF MY RIGHTS...

"LET THE BUYER BEWARE!"

8. Who was Randolph?

(I'm Not Your Sweet Babboo!)

_____

9. Who has naturally curly hair?

(What Makes Musicians So Sarcastic?)

_____

10. When was the last time Lucy was wrong?

(What Makes Musicians So Sarcastic?)

_____

11. Once a new kid moved into the neighborhood, and his name was a number. Name that number.

(What's Wrong with Being Crabby?)

8.

BEFORE WE CONTINUE WITH YOUR TREATMENT, WE NEED TO DO SOMETHING..
I'M GOING TO ASK YOU TO TAKE THE BLANKET OFF YOUR HEAD...
ANYTHING YOU SAY...
IT'S ME, SWEET BABBOO!
AAUGH!
SCHULZ

9.

FRIEDA, THIS IS MY SISTER, LUCY...
HOW DO YOU DO, LUCY? HAVE YOU EVER MET ANYONE BEFORE WHO HAS NATURALLY CURLY HAIR? ACTUALLY, I'M VERY GRATEFUL FOR IT!
SHE'S KIND OF A FRIEND OF MINE, LUCY, AND SHE SITS BEHIND ME AT SCHOOL....
PLEASE DON'T SLUG HER...
SCHULZ

10.

YOU? YOU ADMIT YOU WERE WRONG? YOU? YOU?!
OF COURSE, CHARLIE BROWN.. AND I'LL ADMIT THAT I'VE BEEN WRONG BEFORE...
I REMEMBER THE LAST TIME I WAS WRONG ABOUT SOMETHING.. IT WAS IN 1958, I THINK.... ALONG IN JULY SOMETIME, OR WAS IT IN AUGUST? YES!
THE LAST TIME I WAS WRONG WAS IN AUGUST, 1958.. I THINK IT WAS ON A MONDAY, AND...
OH, GOOD GRIEF!
SCHULZ

11.

HI THERE, PUPPY DOG..
MY NAME IS 5....I'M NEW IN THE NEIGHBORHOOD...
I NEVER GET NAMES STRAIGHT.. DID HE SAY V OR 5 ?
SCHULZ

12. Who wants to have a white-collar job when he grows up?

(Always Stick Up for the Underbird)

_____

13. Who had amblyopia?

(It's a Long Way to Tipperary)

_____

14. What is 5's last name?

(What's Wrong with Being Crabby?)

_____

15. What is the name of the hospital where Charlie Brown was a patient?

(Here Comes the April Fool!)

12.

HA HA HA HA HA..

GO AHEAD AND LAUGH, CHARLIE BROWN! SOMEDAY I'LL SHOW YOU!!

IT'S NOT NICE TO LAUGH AT A PERSON'S AMBITIONS!!! BUT, BY GOLLY, I'LL SHOW HIM!

SOMEDAY I'LL BE A "WHITE-COLLAR WORKER"!

13.

MY OPHTHALMOLOGIST JUST SAID THAT MY "LAZY EYE" IS DOING FINE..

HE SAID I SHOULD BE ABLE TO TAKE THIS PATCH OFF IN TWO MONTHS! THAT'S AMAZING!

MY OPHTHALMOLOGIST AND I REGARD THIS AS A MAJOR MEDICAL TRIUMPH...

WITH NOTHING MORE THAN A SIMPLE EYE PATCH, WE HAVE BROUGHT AMBLYOPIA TO ITS KNEES!

14.

SALLY, I'D LIKE TO HAVE YOU MEET A NEW BOY IN OUR NEIGHBORHOOD..

5, THIS IS MY SISTER, SALLY... SALLY, THIS IS 5... HIS LAST NAME IS 95472..

"MRS. SALLY 95472"

I CAN'T SEE IT!

15.

NO, THIS IS SALLY... I'M HIS SISTER... HE'S WHERE?

IT'S THE "ACE MEMORIAL HOSPITAL"...YOUR OWNER'S IN THE HOSPITAL!

NO, MY PARENTS ARE AT THE BARBERS' PICNIC...YES, I'LL TELL THEM ..HOW LONG WILL HE BE IN THE HOSPITAL? IS HE GOING TO GET WELL?

SHOULD I FEED THE DOG?

16. What did Charlie Brown's medical necktag read?

(Here Comes the April Fool!)

_____

17. What is Snoopy's favorite drink?

(Here Comes the April Fool!)

_____

18. Who did her hair in cornrows?

(Dr. Beagle and Mr. Hyde)

_____

19. Why does Sally want to be a nurse when she grows up?

(A Smile Makes a Lousy Umbrella)

16.

WHAT'S THAT YOU'RE WEARING AROUND YOUR NECK, CHARLIE BROWN?
IT'S A MEDICAL TAG...LOTS OF PEOPLE WEAR THEM...
WHAT DOES IT SAY?
"INSECURE"
SCHULZ

17.

HERE'S THE WORLD WAR I FLYING ACE IN PARIS...
HE IS SITTING IN A SMALL SIDEWALK CAFE WITH A BEAUTIFUL YOUNG FRENCH LASS...
HE MUST IMPRESS HER WITH HIS SOPHISTICATED MANNER
MAY I SEE THE ROOT BEER LIST, PLEASE?
SCHULZ

18.

I MAY GIVE UP, MARCIE...
I THOUGHT IT WOULD HELP MY APPEARANCE TO "CORNROW" MY STRING BEAN HAIR...
I'M AFRAID IT'S NOT ENOUGH...
I'M STILL STUCK WITH A POTATO NOSE!
SCHULZ

19.

I'VE DECIDED SOMETHING..
I'VE DECIDED TO BECOME A NURSE WHEN I GROW UP!
HOW DID YOU HAPPEN TO DECIDE THAT?
I LIKE WHITE SHOES
SCHULZ

---

20. If Charlie Brown could choose his own nickname, what
    would he want everyone to call him?

(What's Wrong with Being Crabby?)

20.

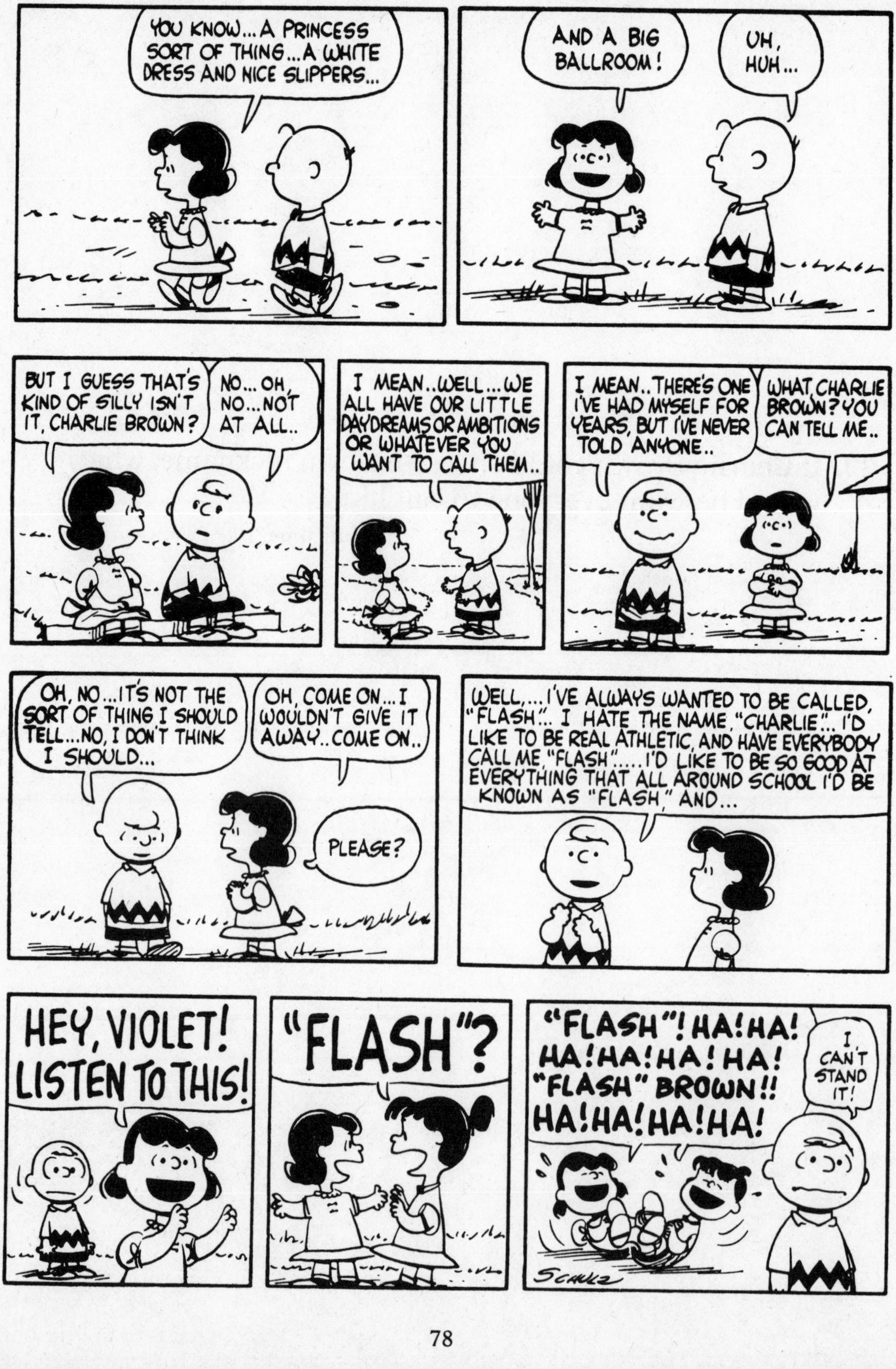
YOU KNOW... A PRINCESS SORT OF THING... A WHITE DRESS AND NICE SLIPPERS...
AND A BIG BALLROOM!
UH, HUH...
BUT I GUESS THAT'S KIND OF SILLY ISN'T IT, CHARLIE BROWN?
NO... OH, NO... NOT AT ALL..
I MEAN..WELL... WE ALL HAVE OUR LITTLE DAYDREAMS OR AMBITIONS OR WHATEVER YOU WANT TO CALL THEM..
I MEAN.. THERE'S ONE I'VE HAD MYSELF FOR YEARS, BUT I'VE NEVER TOLD ANYONE..
WHAT, CHARLIE BROWN? YOU CAN TELL ME..
OH, NO... IT'S NOT THE SORT OF THING I SHOULD TELL... NO, I DON'T THINK I SHOULD...
OH, COME ON... I WOULDN'T GIVE IT AWAY.. COME ON..
PLEASE?
WELL,... I'VE ALWAYS WANTED TO BE CALLED "FLASH".. I HATE THE NAME "CHARLIE".. I'D LIKE TO BE REAL ATHLETIC, AND HAVE EVERYBODY CALL ME "FLASH"..... I'D LIKE TO BE SO GOOD AT EVERYTHING THAT ALL AROUND SCHOOL I'D BE KNOWN AS "FLASH," AND...
HEY, VIOLET! LISTEN TO THIS!
"FLASH"?
"FLASH"! HA! HA! HA! HA! HA! HA! "FLASH" BROWN!! HA! HA! HA! HA!
I CAN'T STAND IT!
SCHULZ

21. How old is Charlie Brown?

(Here Comes the April Fool!)

_____

22. Who ended up with one pierced ear?

(Speak Softly and Carry a Beagle)

_____

23. Who wears a sailor's hat and Hawaiian shirt?

(It's Great to Be a Super Star)

_____

24. What does Linus think every baby should be given at birth?

(Thank Goodness for People)

21.

YES, MA'AM...THAT'S MY PRESENT ADDRESS... MY NAME IS CHARLES BROWN.. I'M EIGHT AND A HALF...

I SUPPOSE SO...NO, I DON'T HAVE A SOCIAL SECURITY NUMBER...

YES, I'VE HAD ALL MY SHOTS..NO, MA'AM, NO ALLERGIES..INSURANCE?

SPEAKING OF MONEY, HOW'S YOUR FUND RAISING PROGRAM COMING ALONG?

22.

LUCILLE, YOU RAN OUT ON ME!!

I HAD ONE EAR PIERCED, AND YOU RAN OUT! WHAT AM I GOING TO DO WITH ONE PIERCED EAR?!!!

I SHOULD HAVE LISTENED TO YOU, MARCIE...BESIDES, WHAT DO GIRLS LIKE US WHO HAVE LONG HAIR NEED WITH PIERCED EARS?

I HAD MY EARS PIERCED LAST YEAR, SIR...

AAUGH!

23.

I LEARNED SOMETHING IN SCHOOL TODAY

I SIGNED UP FOR FOLK GUITAR, COMPUTER PROGRAMMING, STAINED GLASS ART, SHOEMAKING AND A NATURAL FOODS WORKSHOP..

I GOT SPELLING, HISTORY, ARITHMETIC AND TWO STUDY PERIODS

SO WHAT DID YOU LEARN?

I LEARNED THAT WHAT YOU SIGN UP FOR AND WHAT YOU GET ARE TWO DIFFERENT THINGS

(Roy)

24.

I FEEL SORRY FOR LITTLE BABIES..

WHEN A LITTLE BABY IS BORN INTO THIS COLD WORLD, HE'S CONFUSED! HE'S FRIGHTENED!

HE NEEDS SOMETHING TO CHEER HIM UP...

THE WAY I SEE IT AS SOON AS A BABY IS BORN, HE SHOULD BE ISSUED A BANJO!

25. Who said "Cats are the crab grass in the lawn of life"?

(What Makes Musicians So Sarcastic?)

_____

26. Who has forgotten his three good memories?

(Stop Snowing on My Secretary)

_____

27. Why did Snoopy wear a copper bracelet?

(It's Great to Be a Super Star)

_____

28. Which character drew his own comic strip?

(There Goes the Shutout)

25.
HEY! COME AND SEE!
FRIEDA'S GOT HER CAT!!
OH, NO!
IT'S HAPPENING, AND I CAN'T BELIEVE IT!
THIS IS TERRIBLE...
TO ME, CATS ARE THE CRAB GRASS IN THE LAWN OF LIFE!
SCHULZ

26.
WE ALL NEED HOPE, FRANKLIN, DID YOU KNOW THAT?
AND WE ALL NEED MEMORIES... WITHOUT GOOD MEMORIES, LIFE CAN BE PRETTY SKUNGIE...
I HAD THREE GOOD MEMORIES ONCE...
BUT I FORGOT WHAT THEY WERE!
SCHULZ

27.
YOU JUST THINK THAT COPPER BRACELET IS HELPING YOU!
MY ARTHRITIS IS GONE
IT'S ALL IN YOUR MIND! YOU'RE JUST FOOLING YOURSELF!
SMAK!
WHEN YOUR ARTHRITIS IS GONE, YOU LOVE EVERYBODY!
SCHULZ

28.
I WANT TO SHOW YOU MY NEW COMIC STRIP SCHROEDER BECAUSE I THINK YOU'LL APPRECIATE IT..
THIS ONE MUSICIAN ASKS THE OTHER IF HE CAN PLAY THE 'HALLELUJAH CHORUS.' SEE? AND THIS GUY SAYS, 'OH, I GUESS I CAN HANDEL IT!'
GET IT? GET IT? PRETTY GOOD, HUH? HUH?!!
IT'S SORT OF SAD WHEN YOU THINK OF A KID LIKE THAT GOING THROUGH LIFE WITHOUT A SENSE OF HUMOR..
SCHULZ

Sandlot

1. What was the team's ballfield before it was a ballfield?

(My Anxieties Have Anxieties)

1.

HOW SHALL WE PITCH THIS NEXT GUY, CHARLIE BROWN?

WELL, I DON'T KNOW..

THROW HIM YOUR CURVE, CHARLIE BROWN

SAY, HAVE YOU NOTICED HOW BUILT-UP IT'S GETTING AROUND HERE? PRETTY SOON THERE WON'T BE ANY PLACE FOR US TO PLAY..LOOK AT ALL THE HOUSES...

MY GRAMPA SAYS THAT ALL OF THIS USED TO BE A BIG PASTURE..

HE SAYS HE CAN REMEMBER WHEN THEY USED TO DRIVE CATTLE RIGHT ACROSS HERE

MY DAD SAYS HE COULD HAVE MADE A LOT OF MONEY IF HE HAD BOUGHT THIS LAND TWENTY YEARS AGO

TWENTY YEARS AGO? FIVE YEARS AGO WOULD HAVE BEEN ENOUGH!

THAT'S WHAT I SAY!

OF COURSE! LAND VALUES ARE GOING UP EVERYWHERE

LOOK AT THAT PLACE WHERE THEY PUT UP THE NEW SUPER-MARKET..

THAT'S WHAT MY GRAMPA WAS TALKING ABOUT..HE SAID YOU COULD HAVE BOUGHT THAT PROPERTY FOR ALMOST NOTHING ONLY TWO YEARS AGO!

WHAT DO YOU THINK, CHARLIE BROWN?

FRANKLY, I THINK HE'D HIT A CURVE BALL...

SCHULZ

2. What position does Charlie Brown usually play?

(What's Wrong with Being Crabby?)

———————

3. What position does Schroeder usually play?

(Big League Peanuts)

———————

4. What position does Lucy usually play?

(Always Stick Up for the Underbird)

———————

5. Who umpires Charlie Brown's baseball games?

(Kiss Her, You Blockhead!)

2.
ALL RIGHT, MOM...ALL RIGHT...
WHEN OTHER PITCHERS LOSE BALL GAMES, THEY GET SENT TO THE SHOWERS...
WHEN I LOSE A BALL GAME, DO I GET SENT TO THE SHOWERS? NO!
I HAVE TO TAKE A BATH!
SCHULZ

3.
LOOK, SCHROEDER.. THE CATCHER IS SUPPOSED TO BE THE BACKBONE OF THE TEAM..
HOW ABOUT SHOWING A LITTLE SPIRIT? CAN'T YOU YELL A LITTLE OR WHISTLE?!
"NOCTURNE IN E FLAT MAJOR" BY CHOPIN
GOOD GRIEF!
SCHULZ

4.
CHARLIE BROWN, I CAN'T GET OUT FAR ENOUGH IN LEFT FIELD..
THAT HOUSE IS RIGHT IN THE WAY!
I KNOW IT IS.. YOU'LL JUST HAVE TO DO THE BEST YOU CAN...
SCHULZ

5.
I HAVE MORE BAD NEWS FOR YOU, CHARLIE BROWN.. OLD MR. MARTIN CAN'T BE OUR UMPIRE ANYMORE...
KEEP OFF!
BUT HE'S RETIRED! HE ENJOYS DOING IT!
THEY SAY OUR UMPIRES HAVE TO BE REGISTERED, AND THEY HAVE TO BE PAID...
ALSO, OUR DRINKING FOUNTAIN IS THE WRONG HEIGHT...
AND WHEN WE SLIDE INTO HOME, THE DUST DISTURBS THE PEOPLE IN THE TRAILER PARK TWO BLOCKS UP THE STREET...
SCHULZ

6. What ailment forced Charlie Brown to step down temporarily as pitcher?

(What's Wrong with Being Crabby?)

_____

7. Who are the managers of the two teams that play Charlie Brown's team?

(My Anxieties Have Anxieties)

_____

8. When Peppermint Patty and Charlie Brown organized a benefit baseball game, what charity were they supporting?

(How Long, Great Pumpkin, How Long?)

_____

6.

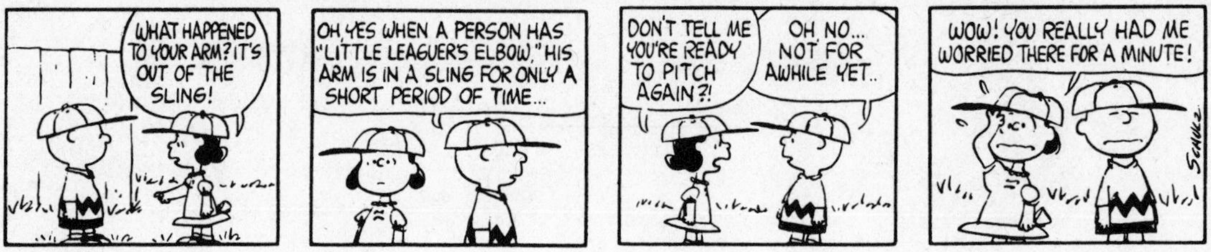
WHAT HAPPENED TO YOUR ARM? IT'S OUT OF THE SLING!
OH, YES WHEN A PERSON HAS "LITTLE LEAGUER'S ELBOW," HIS ARM IS IN A SLING FOR ONLY A SHORT PERIOD OF TIME...
DON'T TELL ME YOU'RE READY TO PITCH AGAIN?!
OH, NO... NOT FOR AWHILE YET..
WOW! YOU REALLY HAD ME WORRIED THERE FOR A MINUTE!
SCHULZ

7.

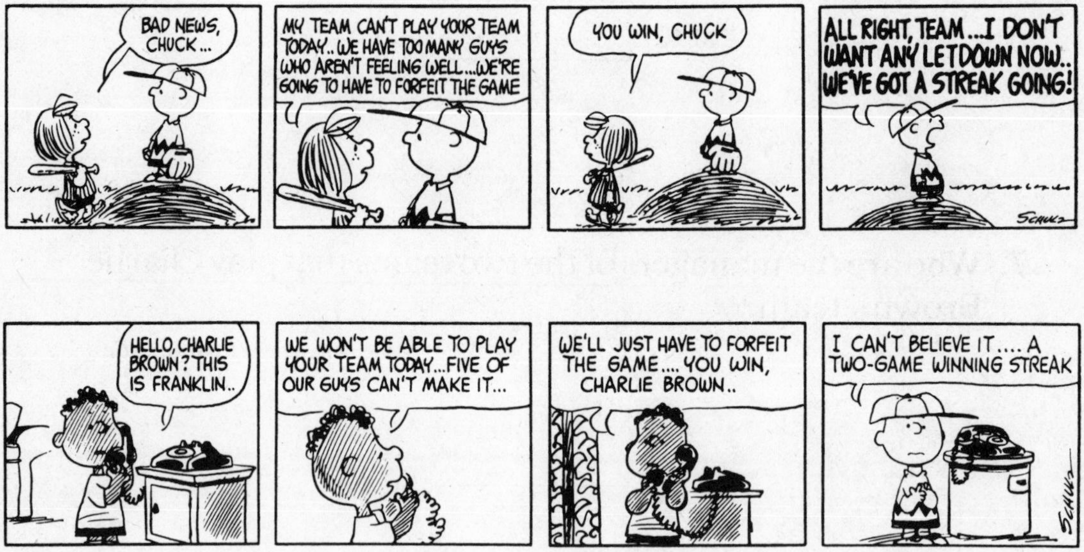
BAD NEWS, CHUCK...
MY TEAM CAN'T PLAY YOUR TEAM TODAY.. WE HAVE TOO MANY GUYS WHO AREN'T FEELING WELL... WE'RE GOING TO HAVE TO FORFEIT THE GAME
YOU WIN, CHUCK
ALL RIGHT, TEAM ... I DON'T WANT ANY LETDOWN NOW.. WE'VE GOT A STREAK GOING!
SCHULZ
HELLO, CHARLIE BROWN? THIS IS FRANKLIN..
WE WON'T BE ABLE TO PLAY YOUR TEAM TODAY... FIVE OF OUR GUYS CAN'T MAKE IT...
WE'LL JUST HAVE TO FORFEIT THE GAME.... YOU WIN, CHARLIE BROWN..
I CAN'T BELIEVE IT.... A TWO-GAME WINNING STREAK
SCHULZ

8.

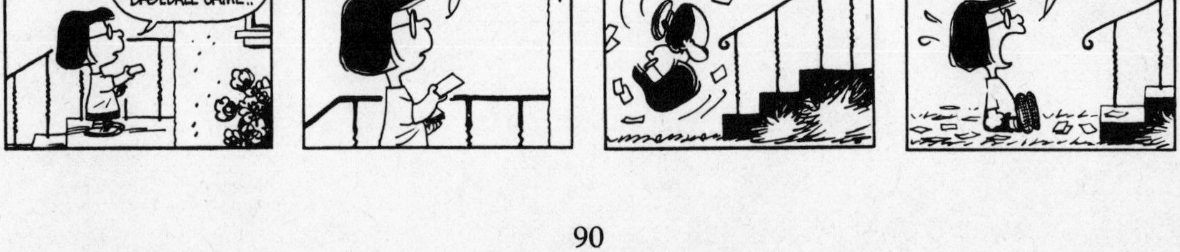
GOOD AFTERNOON, MA'AM.. I'M SELLING TICKETS TO A CHARITY BASEBALL GAME..
THE CHARITY? STOMACH-ACHES!
SLAM!!
STOMACH-ACHES ARE A LEGITIMATE CHARITY!!

9. Why does Schroeder walk the baseball out to the mound?

(Always Stick Up for the Underbird)

9.

THAT'S THE WAY TO PITCH, CHARLIE BROWN, OL' KID!

KEEP THROWIN' 'EM, BOY! YOU'RE DOING GREAT!!

GOOD PITCHING, OL' PAL! KEEP THROWIN' 'EM IN THERE!

HEY, WAIT A MINUTE! YOU DON'T HAVE TO WALK OUT HERE EVERY TIME.. JUST THROW ME THE BALL...

LISTEN...IF THE OTHER TEAM EVER SAW ME TRYING TO THROW TO **YOU**,...

THEY'D **KNOW** I COULD NEVER THROW AS FAR AS SECOND BASE!

10. What player has sideburns?

(It's Great to Be a Super Star)

_____

11. Who is Snoopy's sponsor?

(Summers Fly, Winters Walk)

_____

12. What is the name of Peppermint Patty's team?

(I'm Not Your Sweet Babboo!)

_____

13. What did Peppermint Patty ask Charlie Brown to do to help her team out?

(You're Weird, Sir!)

10.
IF HE WANTS HIS GLOVE BACK, LET HIM COME AND GET IT!
THIBAULT, YOU'RE BEING UNREASONABLE!
WHAT'S THE MATTER, KID, ARE YOU AFRAID TO FIGHT ME?
I..
OKAY, THEN I'LL KEEP YOUR GLOVE!
THIBAULT! YOU GIVE HIM BACK THAT GLOVE!
I'LL FIGHT YOU BOTH! COME ON, I'M NOT AFRAID!
HOW DO THESE THINGS HAPPEN?
SCHULZ

11.
HEY, CHUCK, I HAVE TO ASK YOU SOMETHING..
EVERYONE ON MY TEAM SUDDENLY THINKS WE NEED BASEBALL CAPS...WHERE DID YOU GUYS GET YOURS?
WE JUST WENT OUT AND BOUGHT THEM OURSELVES...
ALL EXCEPT OUR SHORTSTOP... HE GOT HIMSELF A SPONSOR!
JOE'S PET SHOP
SCHULZ

12.
THE MEETING OF THE BOARD OF THE "PELICANS" BASEBALL TEAM WILL COME TO ORDER!
TODAY WE'RE GOING TO VOTE ON WHETHER OR NOT WE CALL CHUCK... I VOTE "YES"!!
I VOTE "NO"
I CAN'T DECIDE
THEN THE "YES" HAS IT!
HOW COME?
IT WAS LOUDER!
SCHULZ

13.
HEY, CHUCK, HOW WOULD YOU LIKE TO HELP OUT MY TEAM THIS YEAR?
YOU MEAN YOU WANT ME TO PITCH?!
NO, WE'RE TRYING TO RAISE A LITTLE MONEY, AND WE NEED SOMEONE TO SELL POPCORN...
THAT WAS WEIRD, BIG BROTHER..I COULD HEAR YOUR FACE FALL CLEAR OUT IN THE OTHER ROOM!
SCHULZ

14. Who is Charlie Brown's favorite baseball player?

(What's Wrong with Being Crabby?)

14.

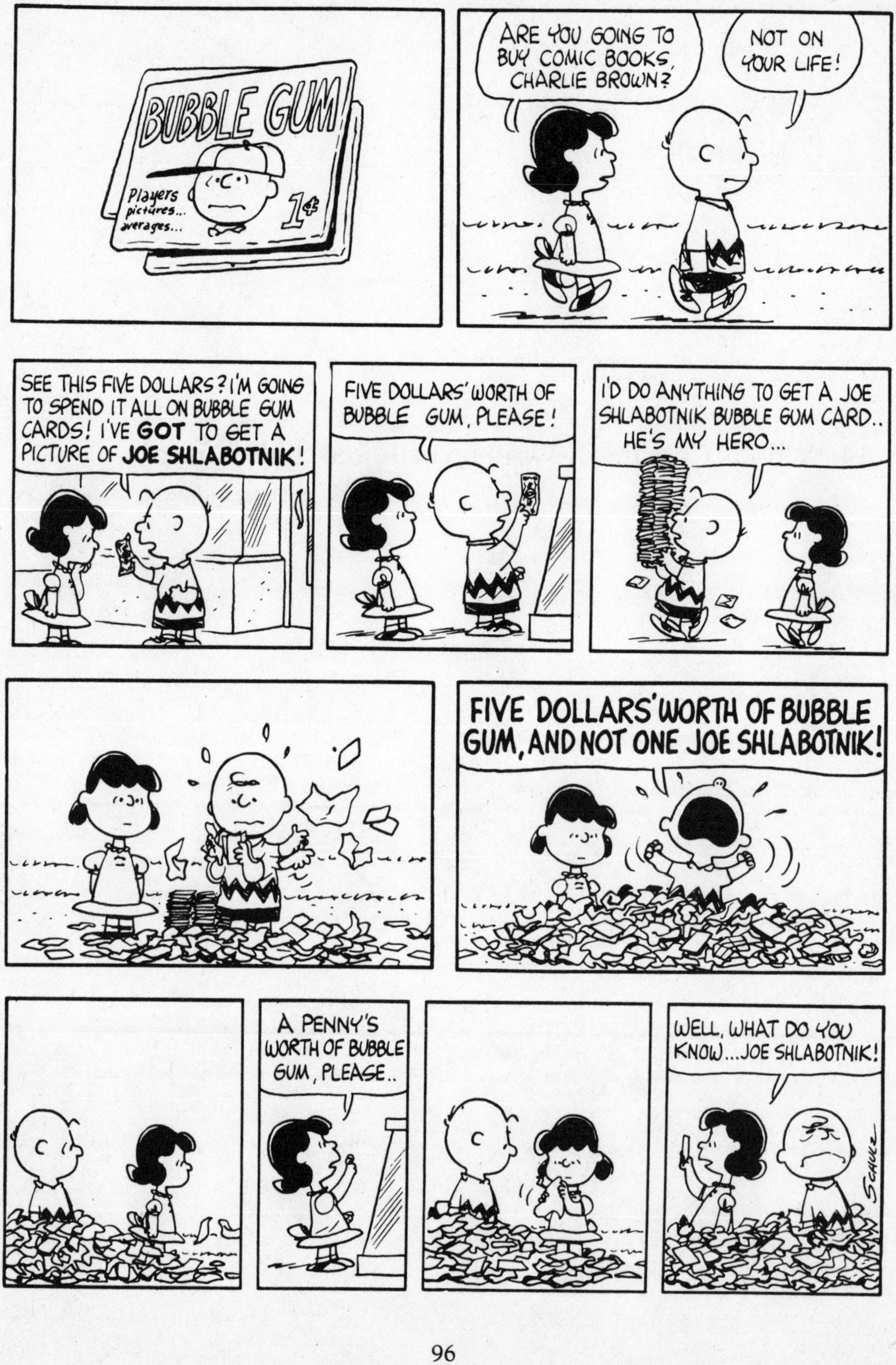
BUBBLE GUM
Players pictures... averages...
1¢
ARE YOU GOING TO BUY COMIC BOOKS, CHARLIE BROWN?
NOT ON YOUR LIFE!
SEE THIS FIVE DOLLARS? I'M GOING TO SPEND IT ALL ON BUBBLE GUM CARDS! I'VE GOT TO GET A PICTURE OF JOE SHLABOTNIK!
FIVE DOLLARS' WORTH OF BUBBLE GUM, PLEASE!
I'D DO ANYTHING TO GET A JOE SHLABOTNIK BUBBLE GUM CARD.. HE'S MY HERO...
FIVE DOLLARS' WORTH OF BUBBLE GUM, AND NOT ONE JOE SHLABOTNIK!
A PENNY'S WORTH OF BUBBLE GUM, PLEASE..
WELL, WHAT DO YOU KNOW...JOE SHLABOTNIK!
SCHULZ

15. Whose autograph is on Lucy's glove?

(The Beagle Has Landed)

———————

16. Who invented the ol' schmuckle ball?

(Dr. Beagle and Mr. Hyde)

———————

17. What is unique about Charlie Brown's autographed baseball from Joe Shlabotnik?

(Speak Softly and Carry a Beagle)

———————

18. Who recruited José Peterson?

(A Smile Makes a Lousy Umbrella)

15.

LOOK, MANAGER

I GOT A NEW BASEBALL GLOVE

WHAT KIND? HANK AARON? PETE ROSE? REGGIE JACKSON?

LIV ULLMANN!

16.

WHAT WAS THAT LAST PITCH YOU THREW, CHARLIE BROWN? THAT GUY MISSED IT A MILE!

THAT WAS THE OL' SCHMUCKLE BALL...LUCY INVENTED IT...

YOU JUST SORT OF SCHMUSH YOUR KNUCKLES AROUND THE BALL LIKE THIS AND THEN THROW IT AS HARD AS YOU CAN

EVERY TIME IT WORKS I GET A ROYALTY!

17.

LOOK! I GOT AN AUTOGRAPHED BASEBALL FROM JOE SHLABOTNIK!

THIS IS THE BALL THAT JOE HIT WHEN HE GOT HIS BLOOP SINGLE IN THE NINTH INNING WITH HIS TEAM LEADING FIFTEEN TO THREE

AM I WRONG, OR DID HE MISSPELL HIS NAME?

HE DID, DIDN'T HE?

HE WAS PROBABLY EXCITED OVER HIS BLOOP SINGLE..

18.

HELLO?

HELLO, CHUCK? THIS IS OL' PEPPERMINT PATTY! HAVE I GOT A SURPRISE FOR YOU! I'VE FOUND YOU A NEW BALL PLAYER....

THIS GUY IS TERRIFIC! HE'S NOT VERY BIG, BUT HE CAN REALLY PLAY! HIS NAME?

JOSÉ PETERSON!

19. What did Lucy's teammate promise her as incentive for hitting a home run?

(Stop Snowing on My Secretary)

_____

20. What did Charlie Brown get in exchange for Snoopy in his trade with Peppermint Patty?

(Speak Softly and Carry a Beagle)

_____

21. Whose gambling caused Charlie Brown to forfeit a win?

(It's Hard Work Being Bitter)

_____

22. Why did Charlie Brown's team cancel his testimonial dinner?

(It's Hard Work Being Bitter)

19.

LUCY HIT A HOME RUN!
OKAY, SCHROEDER, THIS IS IT! YOU PROMISED TO KISS HER..
A PROMISE IS A PROMISE...
FORGET IT! IF THAT'S THE ONLY WAY I'LL EVER GET YOU TO KISS ME, FORGET IT!
ANOTHER TRIUMPH FOR WOMEN'S LIB!
SCHULZ

20.

YOU WHAT?!!
I TRADED SNOOPY TO PEPPERMINT PATTY FOR FIVE GOOD PLAYERS... HE'S THE ONLY PLAYER SHE'D TRADE FOR... I HAD TO DO IT...
BUT HE'S YOUR OWN DOG! DOES WINNING A BALL GAME MEAN THAT MUCH TO YOU?
I-DON'T KNOW...I'VE NEVER WON A BALL GAME...
SCHULZ

21.

A GAMBLING SCANDAL! I'M DISGRACED!!
WE HAVE TO FORFEIT THE ONLY GAME WE EVER WON!
WHO DID IT, CHARLIE BROWN? WHO BET ON THE GAME?
YOUR OWN STUPID BABY BROTHER!
RERUN?
RERUN, I'M ASHAMED OF YOU!!
I DIDN'T KNOW IT WAS WRONG... I'M NEW IN THE WORLD!
SCHULZ

22.

WELCO
CANCEL THE DINNER?
WE CAN'T CANCEL THE DINNER!! EVERYONE IS ALREADY HERE! EVERYONE IS ALREADY SEATED! EVEN THE GUEST OF HONOR IS HERE!!
IT'S ALL HYPOCRITICAL...WE'RE NOT REALLY SINCERE...WE'RE ALL GOING TO SAY THINGS ABOUT CHARLIE BROWN THAT WE DON'T REALLY BELIEVE, AND IT'S ALL HYPOCRITICAL!
I WOULD HAVE ENJOYED EVEN A HYPOCRITICAL DINNER
SCHULZ

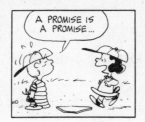

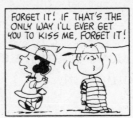

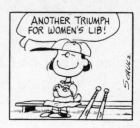

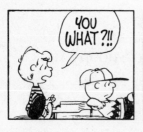

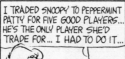

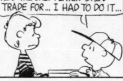

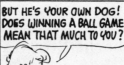

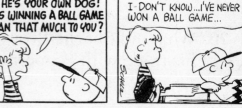

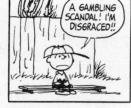

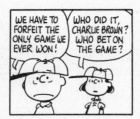

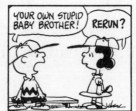

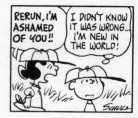

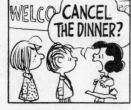

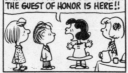

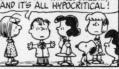

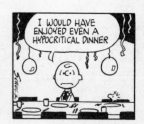

School

1. Who is Peppermint Patty's teacher?

(The Beagle Has Landed)

_____

2. Who usually sits behind Peppermint Patty in class?

(Summers Fly, Winters Walk)

_____

3. Whose teacher was Miss Othmar?

(Thank Goodness for People)

_____

4. Who gets all A's in school?

(Dr. Beagle and Mr. Hyde)

1.
AND I FOUND THE BOX OF GOLD STARS IN MISS TENURE'S WASTEBASKET
I'M GLAD EVERYTHING TURNED OUT ALL RIGHT FOR YOU, SIR...
SNOOPY DID WELL SITTING AT YOUR DESK, TOO..
HE GOT A STAR ON HIS TEST!
AAUGH!
SCHULZ

2.
HEY, MARCIE... WHAT'S THE ANSWER TO THE THIRD QUESTION?
WHY SHOULD I TELL YOU?
3. Why should I tell you?
THANKS, MARCIE... WE'LL PROBABLY BE THE ONLY ONES IN THE WHOLE CLASS WHO'LL GET IT RIGHT!
SCHULZ

3.
WHAT'S THIS ABOUT YOU AND A "MISS OTHMAR"? WHO IN THE WORLD IS MISS OTHMAR?
SHE'S MY TEACHER...SHE UNDERSTANDS ME!
EITHER SHE'S A GENIUS, OR SHE'S NEW ON THE JOB
SCHULZ

4.
YOU GOT ALL A'S ? WOW! THAT'S GREAT, MARCIE! I GOT A BUNCH OF D MINUSES...
LET ME HOLD YOUR REPORT CARD, MARCIE... I'D JUST LIKE TO SEE WHAT IT'S LIKE TO HOLD A CARD WITH ALL A'S...
HERE, YOU HOLD MY CARD, AND I'LL HOLD YOURS
WELL, YOU DON'T HAVE TO HOLD IT LIKE THAT!
SCHULZ

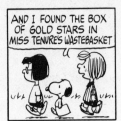

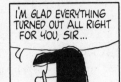

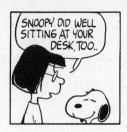

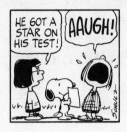

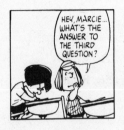

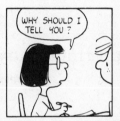

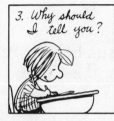

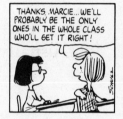

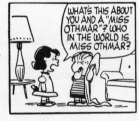

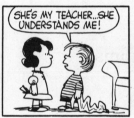

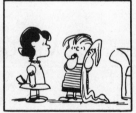

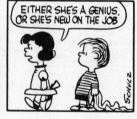

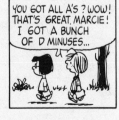

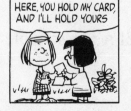

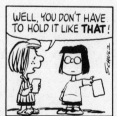

5. What did Linus give Miss Othmar for a wedding present?

   (Thank Goodness for People)

   ————————

6. What is Miss Othmar's married name?

   (Thank Goodness for People)

   ————————

7. Who replaced Miss Othmar when she was fired?

   (My Anxieties Have Anxieties)

   ————————

8. Whose mother puts inspirational notes in each day's bag
   lunch?

   (It's a Long Way to Tipperary)

5.

WHAT IN THE WORLD ARE YOU DOING?
I'M GOING TO SEND MISS OTHMAR A WEDDING PRESENT...
WELL, THAT'S VERY THOUGHTFUL OF YOU, LINUS....WHAT ARE YOU SENDING HER?
A BOX OF EGG SHELLS!
SCHULZ

6.

LOOK, CHARLIE BROWN! A LETTER FROM MISS OTHMAR!
ONLY HER NAME ISN'T OTHMAR ANY MORE...IT'S MRS. HAGEMEYER! SHE THANKS ME FOR THE EGG SHELLS I SENT, AND SAYS SHE'LL KEEP THEM FOREVER...
AND SHE SAYS SHE MISSES ALL THE KIDS IN HER CLASS, BUT YOU KNOW WHO SHE SAYS SHE MISSES MOST? ME!!
SCHULZ

7.

YES, MA'AM? YOU WANT ME TO POUND THE ERASERS? YES, MISS HALVERSON, I'D BE GLAD TO...
MISS HALVERSON MUST LIKE ME.. IT'S A PRIVILEGE TO BE SELECTED TO POUND THE ERASERS...
WAP WAP WAP
WAP
WAP
MY MEMORIES OF MISS OTHMAR ARE GOING UP IN CHALK DUST...
SCHULZ

8.

IS YOUR MOM PUTTING NOTES IN YOUR LUNCH AGAIN?
YES, THIS IS THE FIRST ONE THIS YEAR
"DEAR SON, I WILL BE AWAY WHEN YOU GET HOME FROM SCHOOL TODAY.. I HAVE BEEN INVITED TO A BRIDGE PARTY... I WILL LEAVE A SANDWICH AND SOME MILK IN THE REFRIGERATOR..."
"STUDY HARD TODAY.. MAKE US PROUD OF YOU.. THE FUTURE IS IN THE HANDS OF YOUR GENERATION.. I SUPPOSE IN MANY WAYS OUR GENERATION HAS FAILED YOURS, BUT WE DID TRY... PLEASE JUDGE US WITH MERCY.."
MOM GETS CARRIED AWAY!
SCHULZ

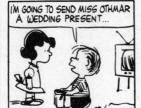

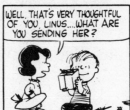

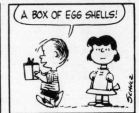

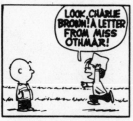

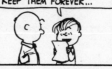

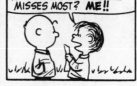

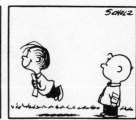

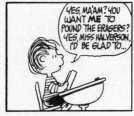

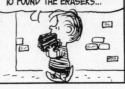

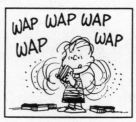

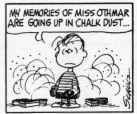

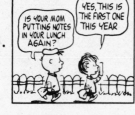

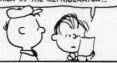

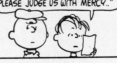

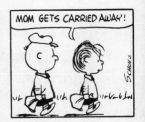

9. Why did Peppermint Patty want to go to the Ace School for Gifted Children?

(You're Weird, Sir!)

---

10. What project of Lucy's won first prize at the science fair?

(What's Wrong with Being Crabby?)

---

11. What is Marcie's explanation for why Peppermint Patty falls asleep in class?

(And a Woodstock in a Birch Tree)

---

12. Where did Peppermint Patty go to find out about her narcolepsy?

(I'm Not Your Sweet Babboo!)

9.

"ACE SCHOOL FOR GIFTED CHILDREN"... HOW ABOUT THAT, CHUCK?
JUST THINK..A SCHOOL THAT GIVES YOU PRESENTS! I'M GONNA APPLY!
ARE YOU SURE YOU'RE READING THAT RIGHT?
THE FIRST THINGS I'M GONNA ASK FOR ARE SOME NEW SKATES AND MAYBE A DART BOARD...
SCHULZ

10.

WELCOME TO OUR SCIENCE FAIR
PLANT LIFE
HOW PLANTS GROW
MARTHA ARGUELLO
Electricity
MOUSE MAZE
A Study of the learning powers of mice
JIMMY HENNESSY
WESLEY REID
SIGH!
THE SECURITY BLANKET
1
LUCY VAN PELT

11.

ZZZZZ! CHUCK, WHERE ARE YOU? CHUCK! ZZZZZ!
WAKE UP, SIR!
HUH? WHAT?
THAT'S IT, ISN'T IT? THAT'S WHY YOU FALL ASLEEP IN CLASS, ISN'T IT? THAT'S WHAT THE DOCTOR TOLD YOU, ISN'T IT?
UNREQUITED LOVE!
AUGH!
SCHULZ

12.

HELLO, MA'AM...IS THIS THE "ACE SLEEP DISORDERS CENTER"?
A FRIEND OF OURS THINKS WE SHOULD BE TESTED FOR NARCOLEPSY... SHE THINKS WE FALL ASLEEP AT INAPPROPRIATE TIMES..
OBVIOUSLY, THE WHOLE IDEA IS RIDICULOUS...
Z
Z
SCHULZ

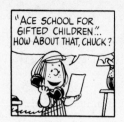

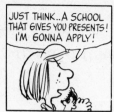

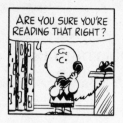

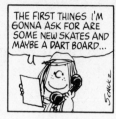

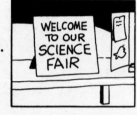

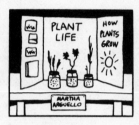

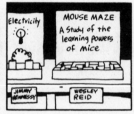

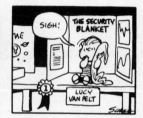

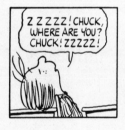

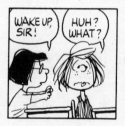

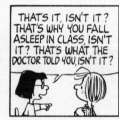

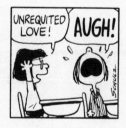

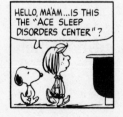

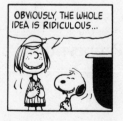

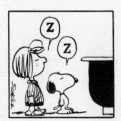

---

13. What grade does Peppermint Patty almost always receive?

(Dr. Beagle and Mr. Hyde)

13.

YOU LOOK LIKE YOU'RE SINKING, SIR...

I AM, MARCIE

I'M DROWNING IN A SEA OF UNANSWERED QUESTIONS...

NOW, I SUDDENLY SURFACE! I SPLASH FRANTICALLY... "HELP!" I CRY..."SAVE ME!"

NOW, I SINK FOR THE SECOND TIME...QUESTIONS POUR OVER MY HEAD..."WHO WAS VOLTAIRE?" "WHO WAS CATO THE ELDER?"

NOW, I COME UP FOR THE LAST TIME... SPUTTERING HALF-ANSWERS..SPITTING OUT VERBS, INFINITIVES, COMMAS...

I SINK BENEATH THE SURFACE.. I'M GONE, MARCIE... I'M GONE...

MARK THE SPOT WHERE YOU LAST SAW ME..MARK THE SPOT WHERE I DROWNED IN A SEA OF "D MINUSES" AND "INCOMPLETES"

ANOTHER SCHOLAR CAUGHT IN THE UNDERTOW, MA'AM

14. What boy got appointed to the safety patrol?

(It's a Long Way to Tipperary)

_____

15. What kind of sandwich does Eudora eat for lunch?

(And a Woodstock in a Birch Tree)

_____

16. Who defied the school dress code?

(Stop Snowing on My Secretary)

_____

17. Who had to take bonehead English?

(Stop Snowing on My Secretary)

14.

AHEM!

WELL, WILL YOU LOOK AT THAT? CHARLIE BROWN HAS BEEN PUT ON SAFETY PATROL! HOW ABOUT THAT?

OH, BOY! EVERYONE IS LOOKING AT ME! IF THIS DOESN'T IMPRESS THAT LITTLE RED-HAIRED GIRL, NOTHING WILL!

WHEN I GOT CALLED TO THE OFFICE, I WAS A NOBODY... NOW, I'M A MAN WITH A BADGE!

15.

WHAT ARE YOU EATING FOR LUNCH, EUDORA?

THIS IS A CHOCOLATE SANDWICH

I PUT A CHOCOLATE BAR BETWEEN TWO SLICES OF DARK BREAD

I OFTEN WONDER HOW IT WOULD TASTE WITH GRAVY ON IT...

16.

NO, MA'AM, I DIDN'T WEAR A DRESS TODAY BECAUSE I'VE DECIDED TO DEFY THE DRESS CODE

I DON'T THINK IT'S FAIR...YES, MA'AM ... I UNDERSTAND...

SO LONG, FRANKLIN.. THIS IS IT!

WRITE TO ME IN CARE OF THE TOWER OF LONDON!

17.

HERE'S JOE COOL LOOKING OVER A FEW OF THE LANGUAGE COURSES FOR THIS TERM

I'M VERY HUNG-UP ON LANGUAGES... MAYBE I'LL STUDY HEBREW AND KOREAN AND SERBIAN...

HI, JOE...I SEE YOU'RE DOWN FOR BONEHEAD ENGLISH AGAIN...

SIGH

18. Who suggested that the school board buy a herd of horses?

(Classroom Peanuts)

_____

19. What girl was assigned to the safety patrol?

(You're Weird, Sir!)

_____

20. Who assumed the alias of "Hans Hansen, the custodian"?

(The Beagle Has Landed)

_____

21. Who is Charlie Brown's spelling teacher?

(It's a Long Way to Tipperary)

18.

I HAVE A SUGGESTION TO MAKE..
I SUGGEST THAT THE BOARD OF EDUCATION BE TOLD TO BUY A HERD OF TWENTY-FOUR HORSES...
THEN, INSTEAD OF PLAYING A BUNCH OF STUPID GAMES DURING GYM CLASS, WE COULD ALL SADDLE UP, AND GO FOR LONG RIDES...
LOTS OF GOOD SUGGESTIONS NEVER GET OFF THE GROUND!

19.

IF YOU'RE GOING TO CROSS THE STREET, PLEASE WAIT FOR YOUR SCHOOL PATROL PERSON TO HALT THE TRAFFIC...
YOU MAY NOW CROSS...
STOP
HAVE A NICE DAY, STUDENT PEDESTRIAN...
I CAN'T STAND IT!

20.

YES, MA'AM..I'M HANS HANSEN, THE NEW CUSTODIAN...
JUST GO ON WITH YOUR TEACHING, MA'AM..I'LL SWEEP UP A BIT AND EMPTY THE WASTEBASKETS...
OH, I'M DREAMING OF MY SWEETHEART IN MINNEAPOLIS AND MY MOTHER IN ST.PAUL!
SORRY, MA'AM..I CAN'T HELP SINGING WHILE I SWEEP...

21.

GOOD GRIEF! STANDING IN FRONT OF ALL THESE ADULTS' DESKS MAKES YOU FEEL LIKE YOU'RE IN A PIT!
MRS. DONOVAN, I WANT TO APOLOGIZE FOR YELLING AT YOU...IT WAS VERY RUDE OF ME, AND I'M SORRY...
OH, INCIDENTALLY.... M...A...Z...E!

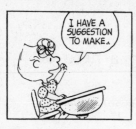

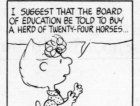

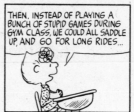

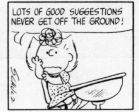

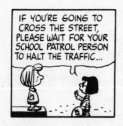

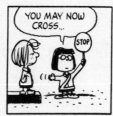

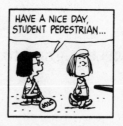

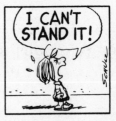

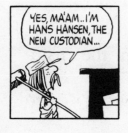

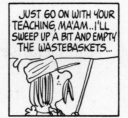

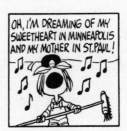

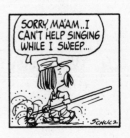

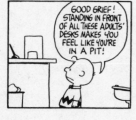

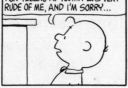

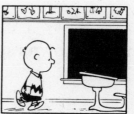

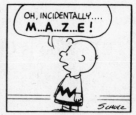

Family

1. What is Charlie Brown's father's profession?

(What's Wrong with Being Crabby?)

_____

2. What was the name of Frieda's cat?

(What Makes Musicians So Sarcastic?)

_____

3. Who was the first character born in the strip?

(There Goes the Shutout)

_____

4. Who was the second character born in the strip?

(There Goes the Shutout)

1.

I HEAR THE PRICE OF HAIRCUTS MAY GO UP AGAIN..

YES, ISN'T THAT GREAT?! THEN MY DAD CAN BUY FOUR NEW CARS, A SWIMMING POOL AND A STABLE OF RIDING HORSES!

WE CAN EAT STEAK EVERY NIGHT, AND SPEND ALL OUR WINTERS ON THE RIVIERA!

I NEVER KNEW A BARBER'S SON COULD BE SO SARCASTIC..

2.

FARON, THIS IS SNOOPY... SNOOPY, THIS IS FARON..

I'LL LEAVE YOU TWO ALONE TO GET ACQUAINTED...

WHAT DO YOU **SAY** TO CATS?

3.

HIC! HIC! HIC!

HEY, LUCY, YOUR BABY BROTHER'S GOT THE HICCUPS!

HE SHOULDN'T BE HICCUPING, SHOULD HE? WHY NOT?

HIC! HIC! HIC!

HE HASN'T GOT ANYTHING ELSE TO DO!

4.

HAVE THEY DECIDED ON A NAME FOR YOUR SISTER YET, CHARLIE BROWN?

YES, HER NAME IS GOING TO BE SALLY! SALLY?

SALLY... SALLY BROWN... GOOD OL' SALLY BROWN!

IT FIGURES!

5. Who sent her mother a Father's Day card?

(It's Hard Work Being Bitter)

5.

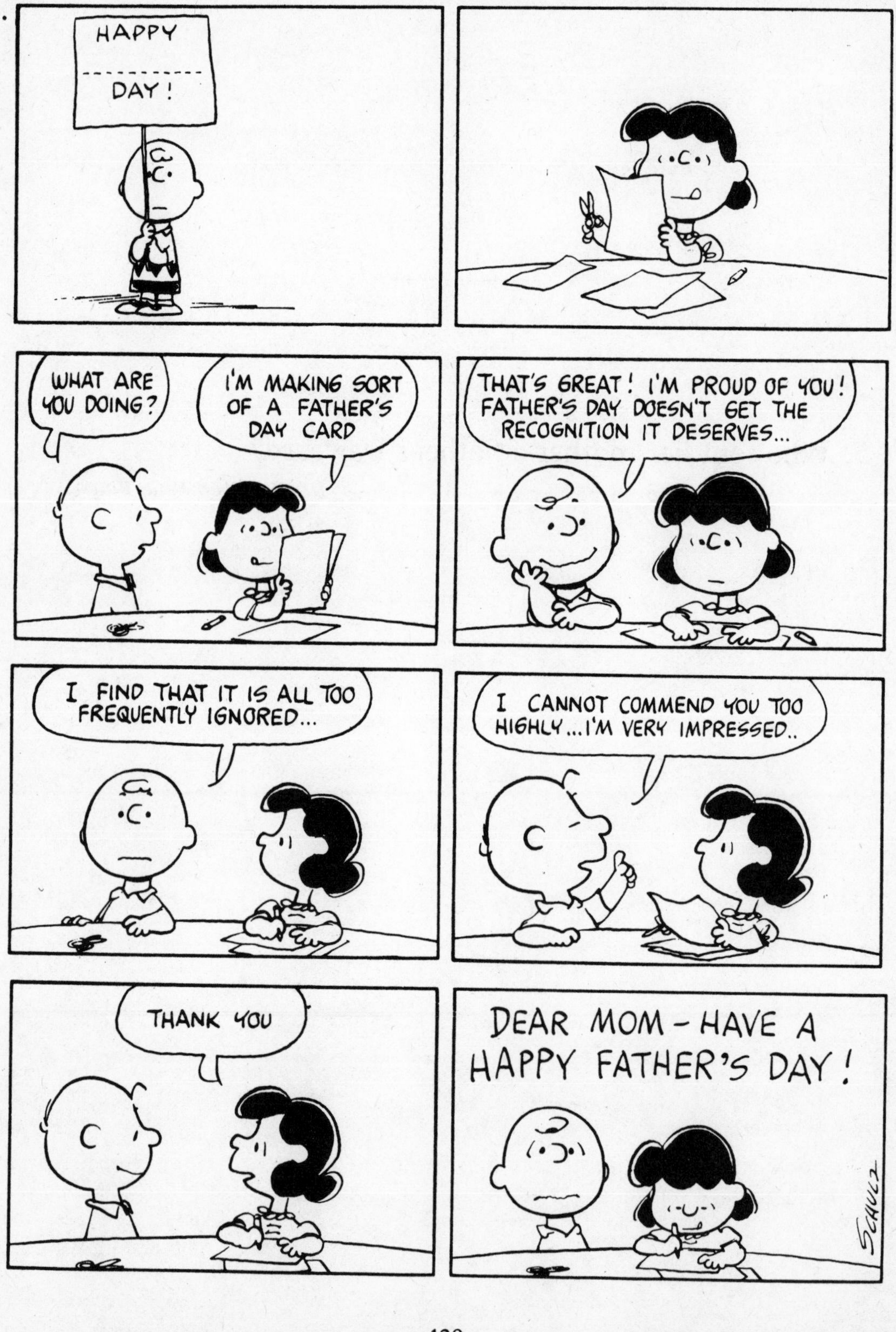
HAPPY
DAY!
WHAT ARE YOU DOING?
I'M MAKING SORT OF A FATHER'S DAY CARD
THAT'S GREAT! I'M PROUD OF YOU! FATHER'S DAY DOESN'T GET THE RECOGNITION IT DESERVES...
I FIND THAT IT IS ALL TOO FREQUENTLY IGNORED...
I CANNOT COMMEND YOU TOO HIGHLY...I'M VERY IMPRESSED..
THANK YOU
DEAR MOM - HAVE A HAPPY FATHER'S DAY!
SCHULZ

6. How much older than Sally is Linus?

(What Makes Musicians So Sarcastic?)

_____

7. What does Snoopy call Charlie Brown?

(Summers Fly, Winters Walk)

_____

8. Whose father calls her "Ladybug"?

(What Makes Musicians So Sarcastic?)

_____

9. Who is the smart one in Snoopy's family?

(Kiss Her, You Blockhead!)

6.

LOOK, CHARLIE BROWN...I DON'T SEE WHY YOU SHOULD BE MAD AT ME...

I HAVE NO INTEREST IN YOUR SISTER! AFTER ALL, I'M ALMOST FIVE YEARS OLDER THAN SHE! **FIVE YEARS!**

FIVE YEARS DOESN'T SEEM LIKE MUCH NOW, BUT IT WILL WHEN WE'RE OLDER...

WHY, GOOD GRIEF, WHEN I'M NINETY-FIVE SHE'LL ONLY BE **NINETY**!

7.

IT'S A LETTER FROM SNOOPY!

IS HE ALL RIGHT? WHERE IS HE? WHAT DOES HE SAY?

"DEAR ROUND-HEADED KID"

WHY CAN'T I HAVE A DOG WHO CAN AT LEAST REMEMBER MY NAME?

8.

IT'S RATHER FRIGHTENING TO SEE THE DAYS GO BY SO FAST..

TO SAY THAT GRASS IS GREEN, YOU KNOW, IS NOT SAYING NEARLY ENOUGH...ACTUALLY, I'M VERY GRATEFUL FOR HAVING NATURALLY CURLY HAIR...I REALLY AM...

SOMETIMES MY DADDY CALLS ME "LADYBUG"....I USED TO READ A LOT, BUT LATELY I JUST DON'T SEEM TO HAVE TIME...

FRIEDA SITS BEHIND ME IN SCHOOL...I HAVEN'T HEARD A WORD OUR TEACHER HAS SAID THIS WHOLE SEMESTER!

9.

MARBLES, MY LONG-LOST BROTHER, IS COMING HERE... I CAN'T BELIEVE IT...

MARBLES WAS ALWAYS THE SMART ONE IN OUR FAMILY...IF YOU WANTED TO KNOW SOMETHING, YOU JUST ASKED MARBLES...

"WOOF!" HE'D SAY

HE WASN'T VERY WITTY, BUT HE WAS SMART

10. Who was Snoopy's original owner?

(My Anxieties Have Anxieties)

---

11. How many barbers work with Charlie Brown's dad?

(My Anxieties Have Anxieties)

---

12. What does Peppermint Patty's father call her?

(A Smile Makes a Lousy Umbrella)

---

13. How many puppies were in Snoopy's litter?

(It's Great to Be a Super Star)

10.

YOU BOUGHT SNOOPY IN THE MONTH OF OCTOBER, RIGHT?

ACCORDING TO THE RECORDS AT THE DAISY HILL PUPPY FARM, SNOOPY WAS BOUGHT BY ANOTHER FAMILY IN AUGUST...THIS FAMILY HAD A LITTLE GIRL NAMED LILA...

SNOOPY AND LILA LOVED EACH OTHER VERY MUCH, BUT THEY LIVED IN AN APARTMENT, AND THE FAMILY DECIDED THEY JUST COULDN'T KEEP SNOOPY SO THEY RETURNED HIM...

YOU GOT A USED DOG, CHARLIE BROWN!

11.

WHEN I'M REAL LONESOME, I LIKE TO GO TO MY DAD'S BARBER SHOP..

HE ALWAYS SMILES WHEN I GO IN, AND SAYS, "HI"

THE TWO MEN WHO WORK WITH HIM ARE NICE TO ME, TOO..

THEY ALWAYS ASK ME IF I'VE COME IN FOR A SHAVE..

12.

HELLO, GIRLS... I'M "PEPPERMINT" PATTY, YOUR TENT MONITOR...

ACTUALLY, MY NAME REALLY ISN'T "PEPPERMINT" PATTY...THAT'S JUST A NICK-NAME MY DAD GAVE ME...HE ALSO CALLS ME HIS "RARE GEM"

NOW, WHAT ARE YOUR NAMES?

AFTER ALL THAT, WHAT CAN WE SAY?

13.

I was born one bright Spring morning at the Daisy Hill Puppy Farm.

I was one of seven puppies. My father and mother loved me.

Those were happy days.

"BEAGLE PRESS" HAS ASKED ME TO WRITE MY AUTOBIOGRAPHY...

14. Where does Spike live?

(Dr. Beagle and Mr. Hyde)

14.

This is your son, Spike, writing to wish you a happy Father's Day.

I am still living here on the desert as you can see by this post card. I have a lot of friends among the coyotes and cactus.

Snoopy and I see each other once in awhile. He has a good home with a round-headed kid.

I could never be a house dog. I like being independent.

Say "Hi" to Mom, and have a happy Father's Day.
Love, Spike

P.S. Please send me ten dollars.

15. How old is Charlie Brown's grandfather?

(Summers Fly, Winters Walk)

———————

16. What's distinctive about Snoopy's brother Marbles?

(Kiss Her, You Blockhead!)

———————

17. What time does Charlie Brown's father close his barber shop?

(A Smile Makes a Lousy Umbrella)

———————

18. Who is Linus and Lucy's baby brother?

(It's Hard Work Being Bitter)

15.

I HAVE A GRANDFATHER WHO IS SEVENTY-SIX YEARS OLD

HE JUST LOST OUT IN THE FIRST ROUND OF A TENNIS TOURNAMENT

IS HE THE KIND WHO HATES TO LOSE?

NO, HE TAKES IT QUITE WELL...

HE SAYS IT'S ALL PART OF GROWING UP!

16.

PEPPERMINT PATTY SAID YOUR BROTHER "MARBLES" IS AT HER HOUSE...

SHE RECOGNIZED HIM BY HIS SPOTS...SHE THINKS HE'S A LITTLE WEIRD...

SHE SAID HE WEARS JOGGING SHOES

WHAT'S SO WEIRD ABOUT THAT?

MICKEY MOUSE HAS BEEN WEARING YELLOW SHOES FOR FIFTY YEARS

17.

MY DAD LIKES TO HAVE ME COME DOWN TO THE BARBER SHOP, AND WAIT FOR HIM

NO MATTER HOW BUSY HE IS, EVEN IF THE SHOP IS FULL OF CUSTOMERS, HE ALWAYS STOPS TO SAY, "HI" TO ME...

I SIT HERE ON THE BENCH UNTIL SIX O'CLOCK, WHEN HE'S THROUGH, AND THEN WE RIDE HOME TOGETHER...

IT REALLY DOESN'T TAKE MUCH TO MAKE A DAD HAPPY...

18.

AT FIRST, I WANTED TO BE AN ONLY CHILD

YOU SPOILED THAT! THEN I THOUGHT MAYBE IT WOULD BE KIND OF NICE TO HAVE A SISTER... SO WHAT HAPPENS? I GET ANOTHER BROTHER...A RERUN!

THAT'S IT!

WE'LL CALL HIM "RERUN"!

"RERUN" VAN PELT... GOOD GRIEF!

19. Who taught Snoopy the ol' Cheshire Cat trick?

(Kiss Her, You Blockhead!)

19.

IF YOU LOOK AT THE CALENDAR TOO MUCH, IT'LL DRIVE YOU CRAZY

TODAY IS FATHER'S DAY... I LOVED MY DAD.. I THINK ABOUT HIM A LOT...

HE WAS THE ONE WHO TAUGHT US THE OL' CHESHIRE CAT TRICK...

YOU JUST GRADUALLY FADE AWAY UNTIL ONLY YOUR GRIN IS LEFT

ONE DAY DAD ACTUALLY DID DISAPPEAR.. WE NEVER KNEW WHERE HE WENT.. THAT'S THE TROUBLE WITH BEING A DOG... THEY NEVER TELL YOU ANYTHING...

NOW OUR FAMILY IS SCATTERED ALL OVER.. SPIKE'S IN NEEDLES... BELLE'S IN KANSAS CITY..

I DON'T KNOW WHERE ANY OF THE OTHERS ARE...

ANYWAY, DAD, HAPPY FATHER'S DAY WHEREVER YOU ARE!

RATS!

20. What did Linus's grandmother promise to do if he would give up his blanket?

(A Smile Makes a Lousy Umbrella)

---

21. When Snoopy went back to the Daisy Hill Puppy Farm, what did he find in its place?

(It's Hard Work Being Bitter)

---

22. What are the names of 5's sisters?

(What's Wrong with Being Crabby?)

---

23. Whose mother bought her piano lessons?

(What's Wrong with Being Crabby?)

20.

Panel 1: I MUST HAVE BEEN OUT OF MY MIND TO MAKE A DEAL LIKE THIS WITH MY GRANDMOTHER!

Panel 2: WHO WOULD HAVE THOUGHT THAT SHE'D GIVE UP SMOKING JUST TO GET ME TO GIVE UP MY BLANKET? I CAN'T BELIEVE IT!

Panel 3: YOU UNDERESTIMATED HER, DIDN'T YOU? / I SURE DID...

Panel 4: THAT GRAY-HAIRED, FOXY OLD RASCAL!

21.

Panel 1: IT'S GONE!! THE DAISY HILL PUPPY FARM IS GONE!

Panel 2: THEY'VE BUILT A SIX-STORY PARKING GARAGE! AAUGH! I CAN'T STAND IT!!

Panel 3: YOU STUPID PEOPLE!!

Panel 4: YOU'RE PARKING ON MY MEMORIES!!!

22.

Panel 1: OUR FAMILY NAME IS 95472... ACTUALLY THAT'S OUR ZIP CODE NUMBER...

Panel 2: IN FACT, THAT WAS THE NUMBER THAT SORT OF STARTED THE WHOLE THING...THAT WAS THE NUMBER THAT FINALLY CAUSED MY DAD TO BECOME COMPLETELY HYSTERICAL ONE NIGHT

Panel 3: MY FULL NAME IS 555 95472, BUT EVERYONE CALLS ME 5 FOR SHORT...I HAVE TWO SISTERS NAMED 3 AND 4

Panel 4: THOSE ARE NICE FEMININE NAMES... / WE THINK SO

23.

Panel 1: MY MOTHER HAS MADE ARRANGEMENTS FOR ME TO TAKE PIANO LESSONS...

Panel 2: I WON'T BE PLAYING ON A TOY PIANO EITHER...I'LL BE PLAYING ON A **REAL** PIANO!

Panel 3: (music notes)

Panel 4: YOU'RE CUTE WHEN YOU GET MAD...

132

24. What did Peppermint Patty's grampa do during World War II?

(You're Weird, Sir!)

_____

25. How did Spike get in trouble with the coyotes?

(I'm Not Your Sweet Babboo!)

_____

26. Who was Snoopy searching for in Kansas City?

(Summers Fly, Winters Walk)

_____

24.

WHAT DO YOU THINK, MA'AM?

THIS IS THE UNIFORM MY GRAMPA WORE WHEN HE WAS AN MP IN WORLD WAR II

JUST THOUGHT I'D SHOW YOU HOW THIS KIND OF DUTY SORT OF RUNS IN OUR FAMILY...

DOESN'T DO MUCH FOR YOU, HUH, MA'AM?

25.

BEFORE WE LEAVE, SPIKE, TELL ME WHY THE COYOTES WERE SO MAD AT YOU...

SPIKE'S REAL ESTATE

"OCEAN VIEW CONDOMINIUMS FOR SALE, CHEAP"

YOU TRIED TO SELL OCEAN VIEW CONDOMINIUMS IN THE MIDDLE OF THE DESERT?

I FIGURED THAT COYOTES COULD SEE A LONG WAY

BELLE? BELLE?

HOW AM I EVER GOING TO FIND BELLE?

THE LAST I HEARD SHE HAS A TEEN-AGE SON, AND THAT WORTHLESS HOUND SHE MARRIED RAN OFF!

"I GUESS I FORGOT TO TELL YOU THAT BELLE IS MY SISTER...IF IT TURNS OUT THAT SHE NEEDS HELP, WILL YOU SEND SOME MONEY?"

MONEY? I DON'T HAVE ANY MONEY!

HE'S YOUR DOG, CHARLIE BROWN!

26.

ANOTHER LETTER FROM SNOOPY?

"DEAR ROUND-HEADED KID... GUESS WHAT HAPPENED!"

"I FOUND MY SISTER BELLE... AND WHAT A REUNION WE'RE HAVING! BELLE IS JUST AS BEAUTIFUL AS EVER"

"UNFORTUNATELY, I CAN'T SAY MUCH FOR HER TEEN-AGE SON"

27. What happened to Snoopy's bride?

(The Beagle Has Landed)

---

28. What did Charlie Brown hand out to celebrate the birth of his sister Sally?

(Thank Goodness for People)

---

29. Whose Aunt Marion says, "Never fall in love with a trumpet player"?

(Dr. Beagle and Mr. Hyde)

---

30. What did Lucy's grandmother do during World War II?

(Summers Fly, Winters Walk)

27.

HERE YOU GOT A LETTER FROM SPIKE..
"DEAR BROTHER, WHAT CAN I SAY? I RAN OFF WITH YOUR BRIDE, AND BROKE YOUR HEART"
"BUT YOU KNOW WHAT HAPPENED? THE DAY WE GOT HERE TO NEEDLES SHE LEFT ME, AND RAN OFF WITH A COYOTE!"
"HAVE YOU SEEN ANY GOOD MOVIES LATELY? YOUR BROTHER, SPIKE"
SCHULZ

28.

HEY, C'MON!
CHARLIE BROWN HAD A BABY SISTER! HE'S HANDING OUT CHOCOLATE CIGARS!
CONGRATULATIONS, CHARLIE BROWN!
THANK YOU, 'PIG-PEN'..
NOT BAD...THIS SHOULD HAPPEN MORE OFTEN!
SCHULZ

29.

MY AUNT MARION SAYS, "NEVER FALL IN LOVE WITH A TRUMPET PLAYER"
I'M NOT A TRUMPET PLAYER
HOW DO YOU KNOW I WAS TALKING ABOUT YOU?
GOT HIM THAT TIME!
SCHULZ

30.

MY GRANDMOTHER HELPED TO MAKE THIS COUNTRY GREAT!
DURING WORLD WAR II, SHE WORKED AS A RIVETER, AND WROTE LETTERS TO SEVENTEEN SERVICEMEN!
TALK ABOUT WOMEN IN HISTORY...
LET'S HEAR IT FOR MY GRANDMOTHER!!
SCHULZ

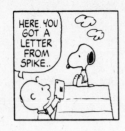

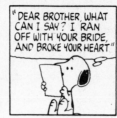

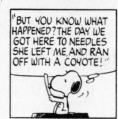

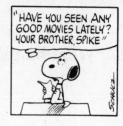

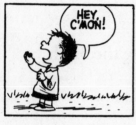

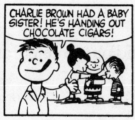

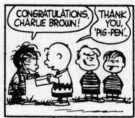

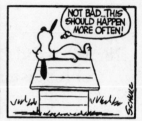

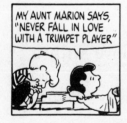

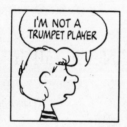

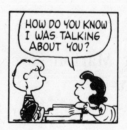

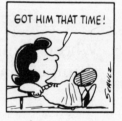

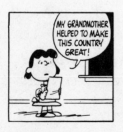

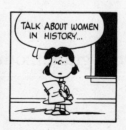

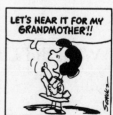

---

31. What are the four classic cars Linus's father has owned?

(And a Woodstock in a Birch Tree)

31.

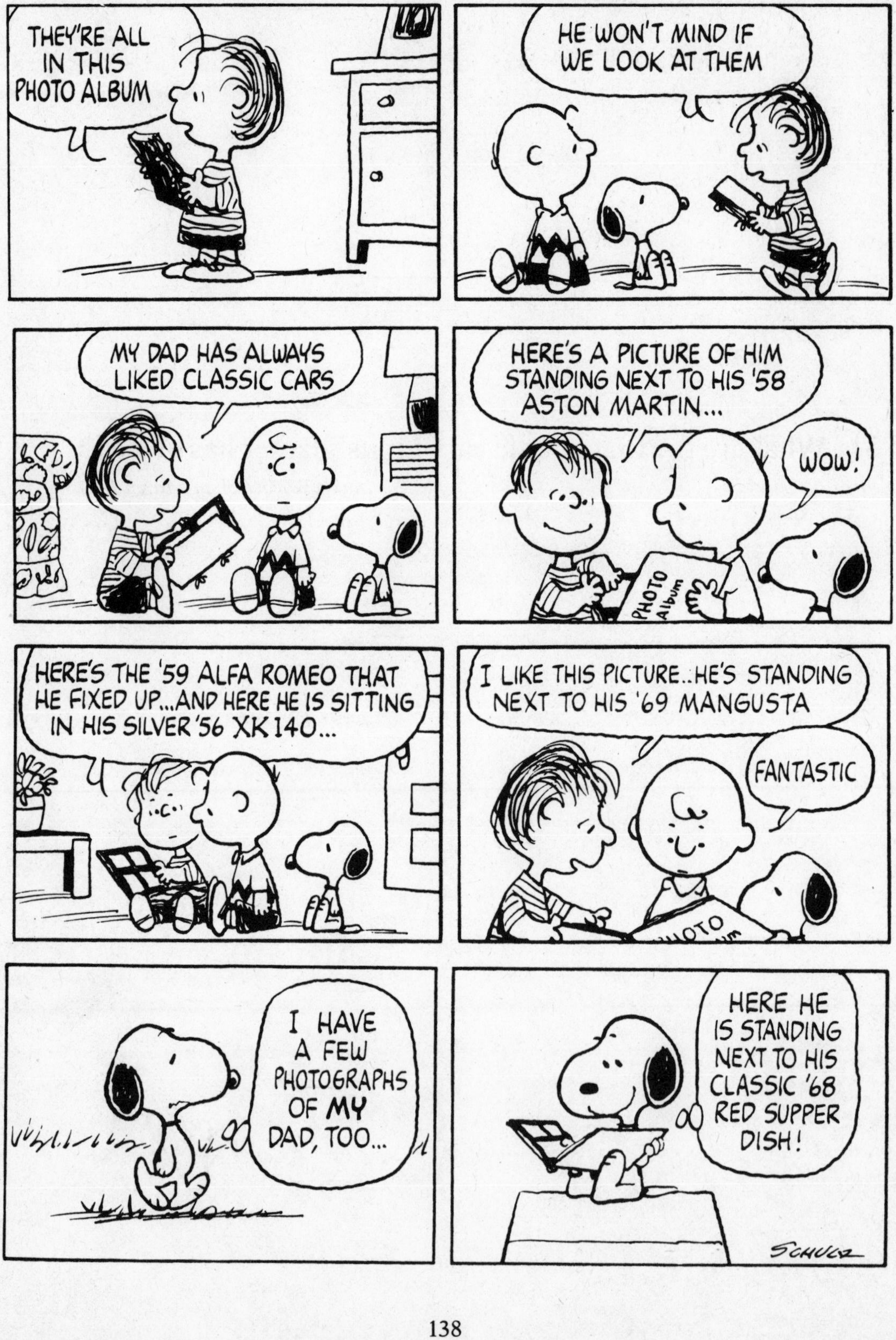
THEY'RE ALL IN THIS PHOTO ALBUM
HE WON'T MIND IF WE LOOK AT THEM
MY DAD HAS ALWAYS LIKED CLASSIC CARS
HERE'S A PICTURE OF HIM STANDING NEXT TO HIS '58 ASTON MARTIN...
WOW!
PHOTO Album
HERE'S THE '59 ALFA ROMEO THAT HE FIXED UP...AND HERE HE IS SITTING IN HIS SILVER '56 XK140...
I LIKE THIS PICTURE..HE'S STANDING NEXT TO HIS '69 MANGUSTA
FANTASTIC
I HAVE A FEW PHOTOGRAPHS OF **MY** DAD, TOO...
HERE HE IS STANDING NEXT TO HIS CLASSIC '68 RED SUPPER DISH!
SCHULZ